➤ Larry Lewin

Using the
Internet to
Strengthen Curriculum

ASCD Association for Supervision and Curriculum Development Alexandria, Virginia USA

Association for Supervision and Curriculum Development
1703 N. Beauregard St. • Alexandria, VA 22311-1714 USA
Telephone: 1-800-933-2723 or 703-578-9600 • Fax: 703-575-5400
Web site: http://www.ascd.org • E-mail: member@ascd.org

Printed in the United States of America.

Disclaimer: Current corrected URLs for all Web sites in this book can be found at
http://www.larrylewin.com and http://www.teleport.com/~llewin. The numbers given in
this book describing the size of search engines, directories, or the entire Web are subject
to rapid change.

ASCD Product No. 100042
ASCD member price: $18.95   nonmember price: $22.95

s6/2001

Library of Congress Cataloging-in-Publication Data
Larry, Lewin, 1949–
    Using the Internet to strengthen curriculum / Larry Lewin.
        p. cm.
Includes bibliographical references and index.
    ISBN 0-87120-511-4
    1. Internet in education—United States.   2. Computer-assisted
instruction—United States.   3. Curriculum planning—United States. I.
Title.
    LB1044.87 .L498 2001
    371.33'44678—dc21
                                                        2001001199

07 06 05 04 03 02 01   10 9 8 7 6 5 4 3 2 1

Using the Internet to Strengthen Curriculum

LIST OF FIGURES

This book is dedicated to my father, John Lewin

1918–2000

who was the best dad a son ever had and whom I miss every day.

Acknowledgments

Thanks to the following people who made this book possible. First, to colleague, tech mentor, copresenter, and old friend Vicky Ayers, who took me out on the Web for my first test-drive and who continues to keep me supplied with timely tech tips; to other Eugene, Oregon, School District tech wizards, Jack Turner, Tom Layton, Janie Stewart, Pat Lyon, Sheryl Steinke, Randy Besio, Bob Dorr, and Lucas Carlson, for years of patient question-answering and troubleshooting; to colleague, book collaborator, and longtime friend Bette Jean Shoemaker for showing me that writing a book isn't so hard to do and can, in fact, be fun; to Frank Koontz, Associate Executive Director of the Bureau of Education & Research (BER), who has supported and coached me into a national presenter; to Internet trainer and author, colleague, and friend Sarah DiRuscio, who always serves as an inspiration; to thousands of teachers who have chosen to spend a day with me in an Internet workshop and who have graciously shared so many excellent ideas; to long-time friends, trusty tech advisors, and very cool nerds, Steven Baker and Deborah Henley, for their generous time; to my former students, for constantly reminding me that structuring Internet assignments is both necessary and enjoyable; to ASCD personnel John O'Neil, Nancy Modrak, Julie Houtz, Gary Bloom, and especially my editor Carolyn Pool, all of whom contributed to and supported this effort; and finally to Linda Barber, my wife, for years and years of love, support, and a shared Internet line.

1

Why the Internet?

In 1994, my school district decided to run miles of high-speed telephone lines to each classroom. The purpose? To upgrade computer memory, install appropriate software, and create a computer network. Why did they do this? The answer is obvious. We needed access to the Internet. What forward-thinking school or school teacher in North America facing the new millennium wouldn't want the Internet?

Yet for the first year and a half of its availability, I used the Internet access only a few times. To be honest, I wasn't too sure how to do it; I didn't really know what was "out there" on the Net, anyway; and I was plenty busy doing other things, like planning lessons, grading papers, teaching class, phoning parents, attending staff and team meetings. . . .

Help was available to me the whole time. I'm fortunate to work in a school district that offered me Internet training opportunities. Even though I didn't accept the training help for nearly two years, it was there. But apparently not every teacher is as fortunate. According to a report released by the CEO Forum (1999), a national group of business leaders:

> Schools are spending less than $6 per student on the computer training of teachers, contrasted with more than $88 per student on computers, computer programs and network connections.

As great a resource as the Internet is, the first exposure to it for a newcomer can be formidable and overwhelming. Many educators experience some initial fear and trepidation; we want to gain confidence in adding the Internet to our instructional program, but we feel swamped by new information and unfamiliar methodologies. Teachers need help from fellow educators who, first, understand instruction, and who also understand how this awesome technology can assist our work efforts.

The intent of this book is to assist educators who want to use the Internet as part of their school's curriculum to support, enhance, and extend instruction. Based on five years of conducting Internet training workshops across the United States and Canada, the book guides you through the task of reducing this formidable resource into a workable and productive supplemental instructional tool. When you're finished with this book, you will feel more comfortable with bringing the Internet into your classroom.

The Internet Comes to School

The Internet uses technology that has been around for over thirty years. Established in the 1960s, ARPANET was a computer network that functioned to keep U.S. military installations in constant communication. College and university researchers then started using this network to send data over telephone lines from campus computer to campus computer, and from there it grew. Computer networks around the world joined together to form what is commonly known now as the Internet, certainly the Mother of All Networks. But not until the mid- to late-1990s did school districts jump into the use of this important technology.

The occasion that sparked the interest of school districts and educators was the creation of the World Wide Web. Browser software developed by Tim Berners-Lee in 1990 gave computer users a point-and-click, hypertext environment on the Internet. "Hypertext" is tech talk for the ability to link different Web pages together by quick and easy movement around the Web. Berners-Lee named this environment the World Wide Web (beating out other titles such as "Information Mesh," "Mine of Information," and "Information Mine"), and the Internet revolution began.

The Web is the part of the Internet that not only transmits text from computer to computer via telephone lines or cable but is also capable of sending pictures, audio files, and video clips—a multimedia extravaganza that allows users to jump from Web page to Web page with a click of the mouse . . . it's "hyper."

The World Wide Web grabbed your school's attention because it turns every computer connected to it into a library. Imagine an instructional resource that allows up-to-date data and information (words, pictures, sounds, and videos) from multiple sources to travel into a school's computers almost instantly. Pretty exciting stuff.

With the benefits of the Web come some drawbacks. Since its creation, the Web has grown stupendously. As this book was being completed (spring 2001), over 1 billion Web pages were available to you . . . and that's only an estimate. While growth is good, of course, because of the increased amount of information that is now available, finding sources of classroom-quality material becomes more and more difficult. No one knows how many Web sites there actually are, and no one is in control of them. Web sites reside on one of thousands and thousands of Web server computers and vary in their content, layout, and accuracy. No single person, organization, or authority keeps track of everything available on the Web, and no one except the creator of each Web site is responsible for making sure that the information available is correct. Web site operators can even post totally fictitious information on the Web if they want to, so the role of the teacher in promoting proper Internet usage in the classroom is particularly important. All that any Web user knows for certain is that every Web site was created by some human being somewhere on Earth.

So the issue facing us is: How can we as teachers help our students turn this imposing, uncontrolled resource into an instructional ally, and how can we integrate the knowledge available on the Internet into the curriculum we present to students?

This book promises to be practical: All the techniques, activities, and assignments come from real classrooms with real kids. The ideas presented are real examples for you to consider integrating into your own teaching.

How the World Wide Web Works—The Short Version

When a person or an organization has some information that they want to share via computer with the estimated audience of 250 million people who have Internet access ("Connecting" Your Business, online presentation), they can create a Web site, sometimes called a Web page. To make a Web page, a designer—known as a webmaster—first must learn the language of the Web, Hypertext Markup Language (HTML). (As an option, the webmaster can purchase one of dozens of software packages that perform HTML coding.) Then, as with more traditional media, the next step is deciding what text to type, what pictures or graphics to use, and whether audio and video files would be useful.

Once the site is created, the webmaster picks a name, pays a fee to register it with InterNIC (a central computer that provides service to a network), and parks it on a Web server (a computer that has a connection to a high-speed modem or a direct connection to the Internet, and which is available for 24-hour access).

If all this sounds too difficult to comprehend, it's certainly not hard to accomplish. Millions of people, including schoolkids, have done it already.

Once a Web site is posted on a Web server computer, anyone with Web access can visit it. A computer (and even now a television) accesses the Web by connecting to the Internet via modems, phone lines, or satellites, and by using Web browser software (like Netscape Communicator or Internet Explorer) to move around the Internet once the connection is made.

Navigating the Web

Of course, just connecting to the Internet is only the beginning. Then comes the more important step of learning how to use the World Wide Web *effectively,* which means navigating the Web to arrive at a site that contains useful, relevant information on a desired topic.

Users have a variety of ways to negotiate the countless number of Web sites to find the desired information. Perhaps the easiest is simply to have a friend or colleague share with you a Web site's address. You can learn about a great site from television or in a newspaper article, journal, or book like this. Educator resource pages list sites of interest and allow you to hyperlink to them with a simple point-and-click connection. You can assign a student to find certain information for you (instructions for this assignment are provided later in the book). You can also conduct your own search using a search engine or a search directory. How educators can start reducing the monstrous informational network of the World Wide Web into a usable school resource is the subject of this book, and we begin our quest in Chapter 2.

___

References

CEO Forum on education and technology. (1999, February 22). *Professional Development: A Link to Better Learning,* p. 8.

The Internet audience is estimated at 250 million in 2000, and is projected to be 320 million in 2001, 400 million in 2002, and 500 million in 2003. From the slide "Internet Use is Growing Worldwide" in *"Connecting" Your Business* online presentation at http://www.as400.ibm.com/campaign/roadshow/extreme/present/connecting4.htm.

2

Taming the Web

All across North America, school districts are doing what mine did back in 1994: spending vast sums to purchase computers, build networks, and contract with service providers to offer students access to the Internet. As I mentioned in Chapter 1, even though my school district took the first step in paving the road to what was then breathlessly termed the Information Superhighway, my busy schedule kept me from trying it out right away. I eventually took the plunge.

My first experience with the Internet involved my American history class. The students and I went to the school's computer lab to locate information on the Revolutionary War.

The session went great. Sounds of enthusiastic productivity flooded the room: "Rad," "Awesome," and "Cooool" indicated that I had found an instructional ally that actually appealed to all of my students. Instead of being assigned the more old-fashioned resources—textbooks, filmstrips, and teacher lectures—the students could just pop on down to the lab and jump on to the Internet for new information! Or could they?

Many teachers trying to instruct students about how to access information on the World Wide Web experienced the following scenario:

Students, thrilled to be "set free" from the traditional media, begin to search their topic. They are amazed when a huge list of Web sites flashes on the screen . . . hours of drudgery and library time wiped away with a simple keyboard command: "What a cinch!" Gamely they click on (hyperlink to) a recommended site to scope it out, only to discover it's totally off the mark—a "false hit"—perhaps due to a misunderstood search term, readability problems, or sheer system overload. After they visit several more sites, reality (read "disappointment") sets in. Finally, their energy and enthusiasm wane. By the end of the period when their teacher asks, "So, what did you learn today?" their faces tell the story, "Nothing—it was too hard. . . ." Energy and amazement have turned into bewilderment and frustration.

Internet users of all ages understand that same frustration; I've experienced it, too.

A Double-Edged Sword

The Internet presents educators with a dilemma. On one side, the Internet provides the immense potential of countless digitized resources to offer students on millions of subjects. These resources from around the world can be up-to-the-minute in their accuracy and collectively represent a variety of viewpoints. Best of all, they are rapidly accessible. But on the other hand, the Internet presents us with immense challenges, such as readability issues, source credibility/reliability issues, and the huge issue of dealing with a mind-numbing number of links that can lead even a skilled navigator off into the Land of the Lost. On the Internet, one of the crucial reasons for its popularity also presents problems: One thing just leads to another. You can start out researching 20th century American presidents, and in no time at all you could be looking at a travel guide for Southern California or a constantly updated photograph from the sniper's perch on the sixth floor of the Texas School Book Depository. Fascinating stuff, but not the purpose for which you're doing research. Serendipity is not a hazard that comes packaged with most other traditional learning resources. But the Internet is different.

As teachers, we need to tame the Internet for our students. To take advantage of the Internet's immense potential as a teaching and learning tool, we must investigate it on our own, condense the possibilities available for students during school time, and structure the experience for their success. We must also teach our students how to tame the Web on their own. I recommend training students to become skilled Web users in three distinct stages: the Pre-Search, the We Search, and the Free Search. Each stage is designed to instruct learners on how to take this vast, overpowering, frustrating, wonderful resource and make it into a usable, manageable, productive ally.

➤ **Stage 1—The Pre-Search:** The teacher determines the topic of study, locates helpful Web sites on the topic, and then directs students to these presearched, preselected, prescreened sites. The Pre-Search is the major focus of this chapter.

➤ **Stage 2—The We Search:** The teacher determines the topic of study, but then releases the students to search the Web for sites that relate to the topic. The students conduct searches to locate appropriate sites. The We Search is explained in Chapter 5.

➤ **Stage 3—The Free Search:** The teacher allows students to select their own topics of interest related to the course or class (still requiring teacher approval). Then the students can search the Web for sites on that topic of choice. Details of the Free Search are in Chapter 6.

By structuring students' training in these three stages, teachers can control the flow of Web use, which is necessary. Many of the students, because of their familiarity with the Internet, want teachers to step out of their way and immediately release them to Stage 3. Although some students have Internet access at home, most kids use the Internet at home more for entertainment purposes. They like going into chat rooms, sending e-mail to friends, downloading games, or listening to songs, among other activities. *Fine,* you can say to the students. *At home it's up to you— and your parents—to decide what you do on the Internet.* But at school, it's the teacher's job to guide students into productive learning situations, not fun and games. The teacher's goal should be to keep the students on track so that the Internet is used for educational purposes.

The Pre-Search

Regardless of the grade level, the subject content, or my students' back-ground, I always begin at the beginning: Stage 1, the Pre-Search. The ulti-mate goal of this stage is to direct students to relevant and useful Web sites as expeditiously as possible. I presearch the Web for helpful sites that can support my instruction. I then check out each site before my students are sent there to be certain that the content and presentation are appropriate. Some teachers refer to this first training stage as the "Guided Search." Other teachers say they are providing students with "Starter Sites."

How do we maximize productive time and minimize wasted time when navigating the Internet? Here are three routes to speed up the Pre-Search.

Route #1: Solicit Colleagues' Recommendations

While I was conducting an Internet workshop several years ago at the University of Oregon, participant Leah Adams, a teacher at Clear Lake Elementary School, showed me "From Revolution to Reconstruction: A Hypertext on American History" (http://odur.let.rug.nl/~usa). This Web site, which is loaded with scores of primary source documents relating to U.S. history, comes from the University of Groningen in the Netherlands, headed by George M. Welling. The beauty of the Internet is that students in Oregon can access this site in Holland in about three to five seconds, far less time than it would take to find all the accumulated documents in a traditional printed encyclopedia (or a whole library), presuming the documents are even there.

Consider also the time saved for instructors. A history teacher can still employ old-tech resources, like encyclopedias, magazines, and books found in the library. And if one school's library doesn't have the needed materials, other schools might. A teacher can drive across town to search for resources, go into the library stacks, photocopy the materials, return to school, and make multiple copies for the students, hoping that the students can keep track of them.

Teachers who want to can still jump through all these hoops, in between bus duty, lunch duty, school meetings, phone calls, lesson planning, and grading. Many teachers are finding it easier to deputize the Web to bring the material into school for the students. What's more, Web sites such as Welling's can be as creative as their Web designers. In addition to the standard source documents, students can enjoy reading—for example—conflicting accounts of the Boston Massacre: one from the British commanding officer, Capt. Preston, and one from an anonymous Bostonian bystander. A few years ago, this access and variety would have been impossible without leaving the classroom.

Other methods of Web site sharing among colleagues include: posting of great sites on the district's or school's own Web site (see Ann Dallavalle, Librarian, Huntington Middle School, San Marino, California, at http://www.san-marino.k12.ca.us/~heh/Library/Web_Folder/_favorites.html); printing lists of useful sites; and joining a *Listserv,* which puts you on a list of "colleagues" around the world who receive e-mail messages about sites that feature a given topic or area of interest:

➤ Internet Tour Bus (http://www.tourbus.com) e-mails me each Thursday a list of five or six interesting sites, some educational, that I can investigate.

➤ Liszt (http://www.liszt.com) calls itself the "Mailing List Directory," offering over 90,000 lists to subscribe to, including 112 on education.

➤ Bigchalk provides eight "top educational sites" (http://www.bigchalk.com/top8/) that you can have e-mailed to you each week. Subscribe to this Listserv at subscribe-weekend@list.nosweat.com.

Route #2: Use Other Teacher Resources

Let's say that no colleague has already found a great Web site that you could use for your particular lesson, so you're on your own. A second route to locating Web sites for your students is to use teacher resources, both traditional hardcopy resources and newer online ones.

Many professional journals and teacher magazines list helpful Web sites. *Classroom Connect* is a monthly magazine that offers Internet lesson plans, articles about online teaching, and many Web site reviews (1-800-638-1639). *Technology and Learning Magazine* tips me off to good Web sites (1-800-607-4410; http://www.techlearning.com), as does *Multi-Media Schools* (202-244-6710; http://www.infotoday.com/MMSchools/). Teachers report that the print magazine *Yahoo's Internet Life* is a fine resource (also see http://www.zdnet.com/yil, and look for the ad for "Y-Life in Print.")

Many online journals are also available to educators. *The Awesome Library,* which organizes your exploration of the World Wide Web, contains 14,000 carefully reviewed resources, including 75 magazines. The Evaluation and Development Institute in Lake Oswego, Oregon, created this Web site, which is directed by R. Jerry Adams (http://www.awesome-library.org/Library/Reference_and_Periodicals/Magazines/Magazines.html). Or you might take a shortcut to http://www.awesomelibrary.org and click on "Reference" and then on "Magazine."

Kindhearted colleagues around the world who like sharing names and addresses of Web sites are always creating and updating online teacher resources and educator help venues. By posting these resources on a Web site, other teachers are only a point-and-click (hyperlink) away from discovering them.

Many organizations have created online teacher resources that have helped me and thousands of other U.S. and Canadian teachers locate useful Web sites. They include:

➤ Classroom Connect's Connected Teacher "Best of the Web" http://connectedteacher.classroom.com/library/search.asp
➤ Bigchalk's Homework Central Teacher Resources by Subject: http://www.bigchalk.com and click on "Teachers."
(Or take a shortcut: http://www.bigchalk.com)
➤ Tom March's Blue Web'N http://www.bluewebn.com/wired/bluewebn

➤ Awesome Library http://www.awesomelibrary.org

➤ Education World's "Best Of" Series http://www.education-world.com/best_of

➤ TeachNet.com http://www.teachnet.com/lesson

➤ Web 66's The Language Arts Teacher's Jump Page http://mustang.coled.umn.edu/Exploration/Language.html

Teacher-designed online resources can also route us to quality educational Web sites:

➤ M. D. Bennett's Teaching and Learning About Canada http://bennett.freehosting.net/teach.htm

➤ Kathy Schrock's Guide for Educators [all subjects] http://school.discovery.com/schrockguide

➤ Ed's Oasis http://www.classroom/edsoasis

➤ Mr. Donn's Ancient History http://members.aol.com/donnandlee/SiteIndex.html

➤ Odin's Castle History Links http://www.odinscastle.org

➤ Marty Levine's Lesson Plans and Resources for Social Studies Teachers http://www.csun.edu/~hcedu013

➤ Dennis Boals's History/Social Studies for K–12 Teachers http://www.execpc.com/~dboals/boals.html

➤ College student Jenna Burrell's "Cool and Useful Student Resources" http://www.teleport.com/~burrell

Sites such as these, which accumulate information and resources into one location, speed up the pre-search. For example, Denise Hayes, a 7th grade science teacher in Texas, was teaching a unit on tropical rainforests, and she decided to try the Web. Although the school's science textbook was decent enough, she supplemented her instruction because the book was not as current or as detailed as she wanted. Denise took Route #2 and visited Tom March's *Blue Web'N* (see the previous list of resources for teachers), which recommends the "Rainforest Action Network" Web site (http://www.ran.org) for a passionate approach to the topic (see Figure 2.1).

One amazing feature of the Web is that it is a different world from one day to the next. Teachers are always creating new Web sites or posting additional information to sites that already exist. As your Web experience grows, you'll find that you can create helpful-site lists of your own, just as I did. With time, you may even want to create your own Web site to share what you've learned or to provide a resource for educators relating to a topic about which you have a particular passion or accumulation of materials.

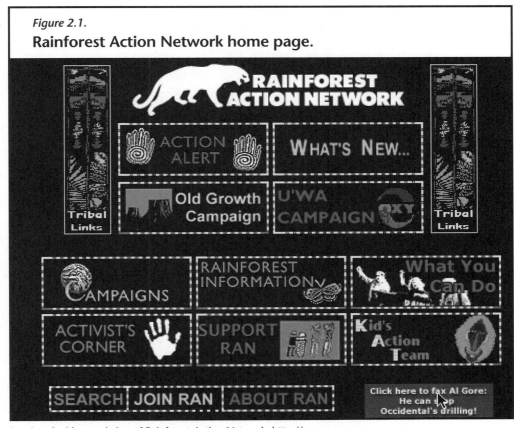

Figure 2.1.
Rainforest Action Network home page.

Reprinted with permission of Rainforest Action Network: http://www.ran.org

Route #3: Assign Students to Do the Pre-Search

Without a doubt, every school has students who know far more about the Internet than their teachers ever will. After all, these students grew up with computers the way some teachers grew up with transistor radios. They don't feel, as some teachers do, like strangers in a strange electronic land.

Deputize one or two of your techno-savvy students and tell them, "In two weeks, the class will be studying [the topic of interest]. I need some Web sites to supplement my instruction. Search the Web for me, and come up with a list of sites you think I can use." Will they take the job? Of course they will, especially if they're given in-class time. Remember to recruit girls as well as boys, and always check out any and all of the student-recommended sites yourself before sending the rest of the class there. By the way, I call this third route to presearched sites "rent-a-nerd," and I use the term "nerd" with the utmost respect.

Route #4: Use a Search Engine or Search Directory

Conduct a search of the Web using a search engine or search directory. Use this fourth route to presearching the Web if none of the first three work out. The reason that Route #4 is the last option is that our goal is to move students to the desired Internet site as expeditiously as possible. Although searches are valuable tools, and sometimes absolutely necessary, the best initial step is finding a recommended or prescreened site. We focus on search engines and search directories in the next chapter.

Getting Students Where You Want Them to Be

Regardless of which route you follow to presearch the Web to locate sites that enhance your instruction, the next issue is: How do we ensure that all students are going to arrive there in a timely and direct fashion? All of us have concerns about students mucking about on the Internet, drifting into places we want them to avoid. Here are five options for guiding your students to the presearched, preselected, prescreened sites.

1. Students hand-write onto notepaper the URL (Uniform Resource Locator, technospeak for a site's Internet address) by copying it letter-for-letter off the board and then typing it letter-for-letter at the computer into their Web browser (Netscape or Internet Explorer). This method assumes that all students are able to copy and type a long string of characters without a single error. One false move in typing a URL, and the user does not arrive at the desired site (although some webmasters anticipate mistakes and have programmed their sites to accept slightly mistyped URLs). Even working from a typed list, many students will mistype an address into the browser. Frankly, many teachers find this method too prone to error and wasted time, so they don't bother with it anymore; I don't.

2. Students highlight a URL from a file on their floppy disk, then copy and paste it into their Web browser. This method is foolproof against typographical errors because students don't need to type. For example, to arrive at the American History site in the Netherlands, students would copy the URL to Explorer, as shown in Figure 2.2.

Students retrieve [Copy] the URL from a word processing file saved to their floppy disks. Then, they switch from the word processor to the Web browser and click on [Paste]. Many of the students also know some keystroke shortcuts for PCs: for example, Ctrl+V for "paste" (see Figure 2.3).

In technospeak, when students use the word processor and the Web browser simultaneously, they are *multitasking,* doing two things at once. In this case, they are using the word processing program and the Web browser program simultaneously. My district's technology guru, Jack Turner, uses a nifty metaphor: He calls it "changing the channel."

This method of relaying the URL to the students is based on all students receiving the URLs electronically—that is, in a file on a floppy disk copied by the teacher before class. While such a method may be no problem in a small-class setting, this process can present a big-time problem if you see 40, 50, 60, or 100-plus students daily. (Of course, you could "rent a nerd" to do the file copying for you. . . .)

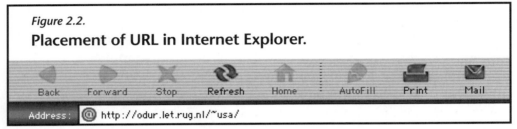

Figure 2.2.
Placement of URL in Internet Explorer.

Internet Explorer® 5.0 Screen shot(s) reprinted by permission from Microsoft Corporation.

3. Students can access the URLs from a file on the school's file server computer. All school computer networks have a *file server,* which is the computer that runs the show. You can save the URL file onto this file server, and then all computers connected to the network can retrieve it. With the file server method, any student at any machine at any time can access the URL, and because multiple copies are available, the entire class can do the task simultaneously.

Of course, you need to know where the file server "lives" in your school and how to save a file onto it. If you don't know about file servers, you probably do know the human being (technology coordinator) in your school or district who does. Ask this person to do it for you, and then save this person some time in the future by learning how to do it yourself.

4. Students arrive at a presearched Web site by merely clicking on the Web browser's list of saved URLs, known as a "Bookmark" (from Netscape) or a "Favorite" (from Internet Explorer). For this method to work, someone must have previously typed in the URL, gone to the Web site, and then marked the site as a Bookmark or Favorite. No problem if you have one, two, or three computers in your classroom that all students will be sharing. But setting up Bookmarks or Favorite Places in a computer lab with

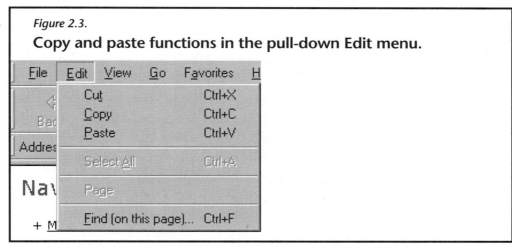

Figure 2.3.
Copy and paste functions in the pull-down Edit menu.

Internet Explorer® 5.0 Screen shot(s) reprinted by permission from Microsoft Corporation.

20, 25, or more computers is a cumbersome process. I only use this fourth method with the one computer in my classroom, not in the school's computer lab.

5. *Students click on a hyperlink located on your Web site* that routes them to a presearched site you've selected for them. This method is probably the best because it's the surest and fastest, but it implies that you have constructed a Web site for your class. The good news is that it's no longer necessary to learn the computer programming language of the Web (HTML: hypertext markup language) because many software programs on the market allow you to build a site with simple point-and-click commands. Even though the Web site creation process is easier than before, building and maintaining an up-to-date Web site is time consuming.

Off to the Web

Before going on to the next chapter, take a look at some teacher sites that easily route students to presearched sites. Go to Teaching with the

Internet, created by my friend and tech mentor Vicki Ayers and me (http://www.teleport.com/~llewin); click on the third link, "Outbound Lane of the Information Highway"; then click on "Teacher-Made Web Sites" (see Figure 2.4).

If you think the work is over when students safely arrive at pre-searched sites, in fact it has just begun. Finding a wonderful font of information becomes important only if the students *learn* once they arrive there. Sadly, many students bog down at Web sites. Reading problems can take over and ruin the learning experience. Chapter 4, "Reading the Web," offers tips to overcome readability problems.

But first, we turn our attention to "Searching the Web." Mastering search engines and directories is essential for both teachers and students. Teachers need this skill for going out and finding sites for the Pre-Search; students need searching prowess when they're ready for Stage 2, the We Search.

Figure 2.4.
Logo for "Teaching with the Internet" Web site.

Source: Author's Web site: http://www.teleport.com/~llewin or http://www.larrylewin.com.

Web Page Construction Help Sites

If you're energetic, and are up to trying your hand at Web site construction, check out a few of these helper sites:

http://www.teachers.net/sampler
http://www.webteacher.org/macnet/indextc.html [in Right Frame
  #2,17,18]
http://help.tripod.com/bin/help/B-Authoring/B-Building_with_HTML
http://www.cyberschool.k12.or.us/~layton/cyfc2
http://web66.coled.umn.edu/Cookbook/HTML/MinutePrimer.html
http://www.ilt.columbia.edu/k12/livetext/resources/wwwdev.html

3

Searching the Web

As an educational consultant on leave from my teaching position, I travel to many U.S. and Canadian schools to present workshops on "Integrating the Internet into Your Curriculum." But when I'm back home in Oregon, I know that stepping back into the classroom is essential for me to keep current with students—both to maintain my credibility as a presenter and to keep my teaching skills sharp. So I contact teacher friends and offer to volunteer-teach an Internet lesson to supplement whatever unit they are currently working on.

Andy Traisman, an 8th grade language arts and social studies instructor at Monroe Middle School in Eugene, is one such teacher. When I e-mailed him to check in, he replied that his class was just finishing reading their literature anthology's dramatized version of *The Diary of Anne Frank*. Since I know the Web is rich on this important topic, I suggested supplementing their learning with a few Web-based resources—ones that I would locate ASAP.

Search Engines

My first step in checking for Web-based information about Anne Frank was consulting a search engine, which is a tool that pores over the Web for information and Web sites that address a particular topic or that contain a designated keyword or key phrase.

Although much of the buzz these days is about the importance of the Internet in commerce and the business world, remember that the Internet began as a way for researchers to share information. For educators and students, that aspect of the World Wide Web remains as the most worthwhile aspect of the Internet; it's an immense set of resources created by individuals, organizations, companies, and governments for the purpose of sharing what they know with other interested people. Caution your students, though, that not all of the information in the history of humankind has somehow been placed onto the Web. Only some of the information resides there. Every Web site exists because some person or group of people has undertaken the work of building it. Sadly, too, some of the information available on Web sites is inaccurate, misleading, and biased. Search engines are designed only to locate information, not judge it for accuracy or reliability. This issue of evaluating Web content will be addressed in Chapter 6.

One of my favorite search engines is AltaVista, which is consistently regarded as a quality Web searching tool. I went to its site (http://www.altavista.com) and typed into the "Find" box my topic, Anne Frank (see Figure 3.1).

Of course, AltaVista found numerous sites containing this name. Anne Frank is an important historical figure; the Holocaust, Nazism, and World War II are also extremely important topics. Many people and organizations have taken the time to create Web sites about them to share information with others.

Figure 3.1.
AltaVista search screen.

Reprinted with permission of AltaVista.

Within seconds, I had a list of 26,634 recommended Web sites, known as *hits* (Figure 3.2). A novice Internet user might be encouraged with such a result, but consider two problems. First, 26,634 hits are too many for me to handle; second—believe it or not—26,634 is not even the complete list of pages on the Web with the name Anne Frank somewhere on them.

Let's deal with problem #2 first. More sites that mention Anne Frank are likely out there, but AltaVista has not yet found them. Why not? Because with so many sites, so many new sites being added, and so many possible words, names, and phrases, AltaVista simply cannot keep up. (Their engineers disagree: They claim that they can cover the entire Web, and that many of the "hits" are actually repeats.) It's not just AltaVista that struggles to keep up, only to fall behind; all search engines have the same problem. I have found additional sites using other search engines, however, that AltaVista didn't find. Remember: The Web changes constantly.

Now for problem #1: A result of 26,634 hits is too much for me to handle. There's no way that a teacher—even with a roomful of rent-a-nerds—could go through that many Web sites in anything resembling a timely fashion.

Figure 3.2.
Result of first Anne Frank search.

Reprinted with permission of AltaVista.

As do many other search engines, AltaVista helps the researcher by prioritizing the sites in order of importance and relevance to my query. Among the 26,634 sites available, AltaVista presents them to me with the "best" and most "relevant" sites listed at the beginning.

Do search engines determine the order of their listed hits by calculating which sites mention the keywords most often, by tallying which sites are the most popularly visited by other people looking for the same topic, by investigating the hyperlinks to them from other sites, or by receiving money from those sites listed at the top? According to AltaVista, prioritization—or "relevance"—is determined by criteria like links, text, and the overall number of hits a given page receives. The company doesn't disclose specifics about their methods because Web searching is quite competitive, and searching technology is an important business secret.

Search Engine Indexes

Was AltaVista able to search within 10 seconds the entire one billion-plus Web pages for a match of the name Anne Frank? Obviously not. AltaVista and all the hundreds of other search engines cannot possibly conduct searches that quickly over the entire Web. Computers these days are powerful, but the Web is way too big a universe for even the most powerful of supercharged engines. Imagine being able to search in a matter of seconds over one billion pages for all the words in the English language, plus all the possible phrases, proper names, and word combinations. It's impossible, and search engine designers know this. So they take a clever shortcut: Search engines search the Web *in advance* of our requests.

Search engines attempt to make the Web more functional for users. We know that there are countless Web sites, plus a new one being added (and others being deleted) about every three to four seconds, which means we're looking for an electronic needle in an electronic haystack.

Here's how a search engine works: It *presearches* the Web before we arrive to conduct a search. That is, a search engine hunts across the Web for sites on all topics, including our chosen one. All day and night the search engine sends out electronic scouts to as many Web sites as it can, looking for keywords, phrases, and names to store into its gigantic database. These scouts are software programs called *robots, spiders,* or *crawlers* (get it? the *Web*). They scan the words at a site and catalog them into an index (database) while recording the site's URL, thus enabling a return to that site. Search engines also collect URLs from Web site creators who submit them to be included in the index. In AltaVista's words,

> Our index is a large and growing, organized collection of all the words on Web pages, images, MP3 audio, video, and discussion groups around the world . . . . The index grows and changes constantly, looking as people send us the addresses of new pages. Our technology also crawls the Web constantly, looking on its own for links to new pages on the Web. Our search engine can instantaneously retrieve lists of Web pages that match your query (12/12/00: http://doc.altavista.com/help/search/glossary.html).

Danny Sullivan monitors the search engine field at his highly regarded Search Engine Watch site (http://www.searchenginewatch.com). According to Sullivan's information, in one year, from June 1999 to June 2000, the number of sites included in AltaVista's index grew from 150 million to 350 million.

Engine	Size in millions of sites	
	June 1999	June 2000
AltaVista	150	350
Fast Search	90	340
Northern Light	150	260
Google	80	230

Nature magazine conducts an annual survey of search engines to measure the size of their presearched indexes (e.g., see Albert, Jeong, & Barabasi, 1999; Butler, 2000). In 1998, search engine HotBot (http://www.hotbot.com) was ranked #1 for the largest index, and *Nature* estimated that it covered 34 percent of all Web pages. Not bad, but the #1 engine only indexing one third of the total number of Web pages is not very reassuring. This fact also gives an idea of the scope of the search engine's task.

In 1999, *Nature* compared them again. This time, they ranked search engine Northern Light (http://www.northernlight.com) as #1, with *16 percent* of the entire Web indexed. Search engines lost ground from 1998 to 1999, but that's much more a function of the increased number of Web sites created than it is the engines' ability to capture them. But when search engines lose ground, we also lose ground.

The lesson here for teachers and students is never to rely on only one search engine to search the Web. No matter the particular appeal of Alta-Vista, HotBot, or Northern Light, always try at least two or three engines, because maybe the second or third engine has located that perfect Web site that the first engine hasn't yet found. So, what are the best engines to use? No one really knows for sure. Many Web users have favorites that they swear by. Many teachers rave about Google (http://www.google.com). I tried it, and I really like it. Now Google is in my top four search engines. New search engines are still being created, too, some of which deal with specific areas of interest. As they do with all other educational resources, the best teachers keep apprised of new developments in their fields. Add Internet search engines to your lists.

Dealing with Search Results

Back to our example. Along comes a teacher looking for information on Anne Frank. He types into AltaVista a keyword or, in this case, a key phrase: the name "Anne Frank". It's important to place the name Anne Frank in quotes, so that the AltaVista searching software reads the name as a phrase rather than two separate words. A key phrase can be made up of as many words as necessary. Without placing the phrase in quotes, the search engine will find all the sites with the word "Anne" and with the word "Frank"—a result that would be most unwieldy indeed.

AltaVista doesn't have time to search the Web for matches, so it searches the giant index on its colossal mainframe computer located in Palo Alto, California, and displays for the searcher 26,634 results. Not surprisingly, "Anne Frank" was way too broad a term for the search engine's database to provide useful results.

Now the trick is to go back and request AltaVista to revise its search—that is, to fine-tune the search query in hopes of narrowing down the results. Wise Web users know that by requesting *rare words*, they can limit the scope of the search. At this stage, the teacher's creativity becomes important. In refining a search, art meets science.

What additional words would you type in to narrow and improve a search for information about Anne Frank? Did you think of "Holocaust"? That's a good start, so how do you add it to the search request?

Using the "Help" button, you can learn how to narrow a search on AltaVista (see the far right of Figure 3.1 on page 21 for the AltaVista screen). By clicking on "Help," AltaVista links the user to a tutorial with search tips, including "+" and "-" signs: "+" adds a given word, "-" subtracts a given word. This protocol is common for most search engines. Plus signs before *both* of your terms will lead you to sites that include both words or phrases. A minus sign before a word will lead you to sites without that word. For example, if you specified a search for Volkswagen - Jetta, you'd locate sites that have the word "Volkswagen," but not the word "Jetta."

So to narrow my search I typed in a "+" sign before "Holocaust" to add it to "Anne Frank" (leaving space before "Holocaust" as instructed by AltaVista, but leaving one space between the entries; see Figure 3.3).

The results surprised me: *324,485* Web sites found.

What happened? Instead of narrowing my search, the additional term *expanded* it nearly tenfold! What happened was that I was supposed to place a "+" in front of *both* search terms. AltaVista writes in its Help "Search Cheat Sheet": Finds only documents that contain both words. Be sure there is no space between the plus sign and the word (http://doc. altavista.com/help/search/search_cheat.html).

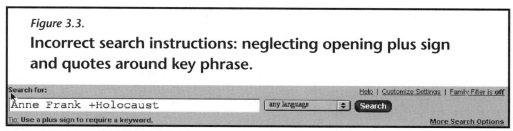

Reprinted with permission of AltaVista.

In fact, AltaVista shows an example of how to conduct a proper search using this method. Just beneath the search bar, as shown in Figure 3.4, is an example of using "+" signs correctly.

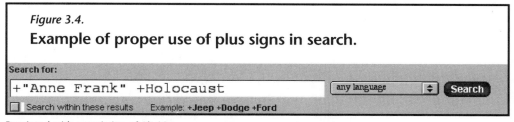

Reprinted with permission of AltaVista.

So I tried the search again, this time with plus signs before both the terms to be searched: +"Anne Frank" +Holocaust (see Figure 3.5). Searching for +"Anne Frank" +Holocaust provides much better, but still huge, results: 9,107 hits.

AltaVista also offers additional help beneath the number of hits. Clicking on the links listed under "Related Searches" and "See reviewed sites in" helps narrow the search for me (Figure 3.6).

The preceding discussion of AltaVista is not meant to be an endorsement for or against using that service, which is just one of many quality search engines that are available. Most search engines operate in basically the same fashion, and the good ones will have an easily understood "Help" function available online.

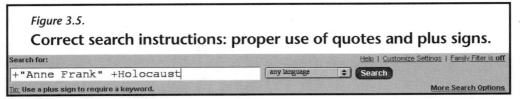

Figure 3.5.
Correct search instructions: proper use of quotes and plus signs.

Reprinted with permission of AltaVista.

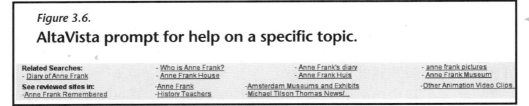

Figure 3.6.
AltaVista prompt for help on a specific topic.

Reprinted with permission of AltaVista.

Building a Web Lesson

While browsing the Web and constructing the online lesson about Anne Frank, I made a mental connection that held instructional potential. Years ago, I had purchased through a book club a copy of *Zlata's Diary: A Child's Life in Sarajevo,* by 13-year-old Zlata Filipovic (Scholastic, 1994). Zlata was a victim of the horrendous shelling of Sarajevo during the war in Bosnia. Like Anne Frank, whom she learned about in school, Zlata kept a diary of her life that was published.

I recognized that Anne Frank and Zlata Filipovic had much in common, and that a comparison of their experiences would enrich 8th graders' learning. But I had only one copy of *Zlata's Diary,* I couldn't quickly buy copies, nor could I legally photocopy the entire diary to distribute to students; so I deputized the Web. With the Web my computer becomes a library . . . an extensive, mind-blowing library that needs taming.

I went to the HotBot search engine (http://www.hotbot.com) for help. Why HotBot? Because I have had very good results with it in the past, and because at the time of my exercise it was highly ranked with an extensive index. I typed in my search keyword: Zlata (see Figure 3.7).

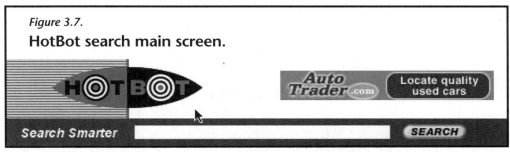

Figure 3.7.
HotBot search main screen.

Note: When conducting a search, users will see in the area where the URL is typed the internal commands that the search engines use to direct its robots through the index. For "Zlata," the HotBot command was ?MT=Zlata&SM=MC&DV=0&LG=any&DC= 10&DE=2&clickSrc =search&_v=2&OPs=MDRTP. (Any questions? Don't worry—such codes do not affect your search.)

Off to the Web

If you want to compare another search engine to AltaVista, try Google (http://google.com) and see if it works for you. Be sure to click first on "All about Google" and then on "Search Tips" at the bottom of the page to see any particular information that you'll need to use Google, then type in the keywords. Compare Google to a few other search engines of your choice. Use the same keyword(s) for a consistent comparison. Find the ones that best suit your search style, and happy hunting!

The results of the search for Zlata were not as helpful as I thought they would be. I figured the word (name) "Zlata" is rare, so a one-word search would be perfect. But that name is more common than I knew: HotBot found "more than 1,000" hits, as shown in Figure 3.8 (p. 32).

From the first ten results that HotBot provided, here's how they applied to my desire to provide these 8th graders with a Significant Educational Moment linking the Zlata of my past to Anne Frank:

Hit #1   Refers to another Zlata.
Hit #2   A good match. HotBot hyperlinked me to a relevant Web site.
Hit #3   Yet another Zlata.
Hit #4   Right Zlata, but I can't read French.
Hit #5   Still another Zlata.
Hit #6   See Zlata from Hit #3.
Hit #7   I didn't understand it, something about Radio Prague.
Hit #8   Right Zlata again, but I can't read Italian either.
Hit #9   Looks okay.
Hit #10   Seems to be about the Czech equivalent of NASCAR. Fascinating, but . . .

I know that I'm not the only Web searcher frustrated with a search resulting in some "false hits." Sometimes even two applicable hits out of 10 seems like a good day. But we shouldn't get frustrated; we should get smarter and try again.

Time to narrow the search by refining it. I added the word "diary" to the word (name) "Zlata" to eliminate (presumably) sites about other Zlatas. Now I'm commanding HotBot to locate sites in its index that have *both words*. I figured that HotBot uses the same "+" signs as AltaVista, so the search request is for +Zlata +diary.

Figure 3.9 (p. 34) shows the top ten hits—every one of them a winner. Adding +diary to the search helped HotBot to help me.

After seeing the results of the new search, I knew I had found what I needed. Look at Figure 3.9 and you'll even see some teacher resources there. But it turns out that I didn't need the "+" signs. HotBot's "Help" button, linking to "Basic Search," indicates that HotBot works differently than AltaVista. HotBot offers a "Look for" pulldown menu with choices including "all the words," which is the equivalent of "+" signs (see Figure 3.10, p. 37). Thanks, HotBot.

The lesson here is that if you are new to using a particular search engine, go to their tutorial first and find out the best way to use that particular search engine. Knowing the search rules before you use a Web site search engine makes your Internet time more productive, which—as you'll remember—is our goal.

Expanding the Search with Another Search Engine

Having used AltaVista and HotBot, the time came to try Google (http://www.google.com). Google loads rapidly onto a computer screen, because the company that provides this service decided not to be a "portal"—that is, an entrance to the World Wide Web (see Figure 3.11, p. 38). Many other search engines are portals, which present not only the capability to search their index but also links to other Web sites offering products, the weather, sports, news, etc. Portals want to be your gateway to the World Wide Web, but all the extra stuff that comes with portals crowds the page, slows loading time, and—in the opinions of many users—overcommercializes the Web.

Some of the "hits" were in languages I do not read. Fortunately, Google offers to customize your language preferences. Click on "All About Google," "Search Tips," and then "Personalizing Google." Or go directly to http://www.google.com/preferences (see Figure 3.12, p. 40).

Of the 10 hits shown in Figure 3.12, three were solid matches. To narrow the search, I added the word "diary." The "Search Tips" help button taught me to connect the words with "and"—meaning no "+" signs are needed—although I had already done my search when I discovered this bit of Google protocol (see Figure 3.13, p. 41).

Figure 3.8.

Results of first Zlata search.

WEB RESULTS   more than 1,000   **1 - 10**   next **>>**

Get the Top 3 sites for "Zlata"

1. Zlata Koruna
Reviews on Zlata Koruna written by consumers at Epinions.com.
http://www.epinions.com/trvl-attract-Zlata_Koruna_12.html
More like this: Home & Family/ Consumers/ Consumer Information/ Product Revie
Regions/ Europe/ Czech_Republic/ Zlata_Koruna

2. Zlata Filipovic
Zlata Filipovic Zlata wrote her diary over a two year period from Septer
to October 1993. Zlata and her parents are of mixed ethnic heritage. "T
March 24, 1992. The Blue Helmets [UN] have arrived in Sarajevo. We'r
now. Daddy...
4/25/2000   http://geog.gmu.edu/projects/bosnia/people/zlata.html
See results from this site only.

3. Zlata lyze 2000 - Golden Ski 2000
Zlata lyze - Golden SKI
1/16/2000   http://www.pvtnet.cz/www/goldenski
See results from this site only.

4. Zlata FILIPOVIC
Zlata FILIPOVIC Je rends, aujourd'hui, hommage à cette fille qui à vécu
au milieu de cette guerre qu'était celle de Sarajevo. Elle a perdu plusieu
amies, autant humains qu'animaux, qui la réconfortait pendant tous ces
moments...
4/26/1997   http://www.district-parthenay.fr/photos/pagesperso/karl/zlata.html
See results from this site only.

5. Zlata lisica
English version Na svidenje na Mariborskem Pohorju 6. in 7. januarja 2
37. Zlati lisici! Zmagovalke slaloma, 6. januar 2000 Teksti: Uro Mencing
Bogdan Zelnik [Nazaj na prvo stran] [Pozdrav] [Program] [Rezulta
Organizator.
4/25/2000   http://www.goldenfox.com/
See results from this site only.

6. Sponzori - Zlata lyze 2000
Zlata lyze - Golden SKI
1/16/2000   http://www.goldenski.cz/sponzori.htm
See results from this site only.

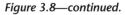

Figure 3.8—continued.

Results of first Zlata search.

7. Zlata Studne
Zlata Studne / Golden Well RP's Home * Royal Mile RP's Home * Royal
Copyright 1997 Radio Prague All Rights Reserved Document
URL:http://www.radio.cz/sites/ Contact info: Radio Prague, Vinohradskå
12099 Prague 2, the Czech Republic tel ..
7/1/1999 http://www.radio.cz/pictures/studne-eng.html
See results from this site only.

8. Zlata Filipovic
Zlata Filipovic Dal diario di Zlata, 12 anni, Serajevo, 29 giugno 1992 Ca
NOIA!! SPARI!! GRANATE!! MORTI!! DISPERAZIONE!! FAME!! DOLORE!!
Questa è la mia vita, la vita di un innocente ragazzina di undici anni!! Ur
senza...
3/30/1999 http://provincia.asti.it/resistenza/pace18.htm
See results from this site only.

9. Zlata Filipovic
Zlata Filipovic http://mediafilter.org/SJ/Pages/October.26.1998.09.12.2
of this page is Ludmilla user4.revere.mec.edu. If you have any informa
Zlata Filipovic could you please send it to me. Thank You, Ludmilla Go T
Main...
10/26/1998 http://mediafilter.org/sj/Pages/October.26.1998.09.12.22
See results from this site only.

10. Speedway
SPEEDWAY WEEKEND 1. 10. - 3. 10. 1999 51. Zlata prilba CS-Zivnoster
pojistovny Grand Prix Challenge 25. Zlata stuha PROGRAM Patek 1. 10.
Trenink Challenge MS 15:00 25. Zlata stuha Junioru-- Sobota 2. 10.12::
Challenge MS 15:30 Trenink...
8/31/1999 http://www.speedway.cz/
See results from this site only.

Figure 3.9.

Results of a narrowed Zlata search.

WEB RESULTS Top 10 Matches   next **>>**

1. Review -- 'Zlata's Diary: A Child's Life In Sarajevo'
This World Wide Web site is the on-line version of the international
student-produced magazine, AN END TO INTOLERANCE, for June 1997.
result of the international
http://www.igc.apc.org/iearn/hgp/aeti/aeti-1997/zlatas-diary.html
See results from this site only.

2. Teaching from a Student's Perspective
In eighth grade at Cold Spring Harbor, students spend a portion of the
learning about the Holocaust. In social studies class they learn about it
historical point of
http://www.igc.apc.org/iearn/hgp/aeti/1995-student-on-teaching.html
See results from this site only.

3. TEACHERS HELPING TEACHERS
This is a lesson to connect students with an understanding of how huma
have evolved in the U.S. It works very well with Black History Month.
MATERIALS: book: The Story of
http://www.pacificnet.net/~mandel/SocialStudies.html
See results from this site only.

4. SmartGirl: Luc's "Zlata's Diary: A Child's Life in Sarajevo" re
Review of Zlata's Diary: A Child's Life in Sarajevo book by SmartGirl m
Luc
http://www.smartgirl.com/pages/books/zlataluc.html
See results from this site only.

5. Zlata¿s Diary
American is generally known across many nations for its popular cultur
people in other countries aim to have much of what resembles America
popular, hip, cool, and trendy.
http://www.unc.edu/~dcderosa/STUDENTPAPERS/childrenbattles/zlataamy.htm
See results from this site only.

6. Zlata's Diary: A Child's Life in Sarajevo
Zlata Filipovic of Sarajevo began keeping her diary in 1991, just before
eleventh birthday. Ebullient and accomplished, Zlata recorded the swirl
activities she avidly
http://users.aol.com/bosfranc/zlata.htm
See results from this site only.

Figure 3.9—continued.

Results of a narrowed Zlata search.

7. SmartGirl: Chloe's "Zlata's Diary: A Child's Life in Sarajevo"
Review of Zlata's Diary: A Child's Life in Sarajevo book by SmartGirl m
Chloe
http://www.smartgirl.com/pages/books/zlatachloe.html
See results from this site only.

8. The Diary Project
Thanks for your feedback both in favor of and not in favor of the monit
entries and comments posted on this site. We were blown away by the
decided to come to the site
http://www.diaryproject.com/
See results from this site only.

9. http://www.rigby.heinemann.com.au/hot/zlata.htm
In 1991, Zlata Filipovic was an only child living with her parents in Sara
Yugoslavia. Shortly before her eleventh birthday, Zlata began a diary.
about her family,
http://www.rigby.heinemann.com.au/hot/zlata.htm
See results from this site only.

10. http://www3.product-listings.com/index/0140242058
by Zlata Filipovic, Christina Pribichevich-Zoric (Translator), Janine Di Gi
(Introduction) Reviews/information (USA) Reviews/information (UK) FR
Web Space ->
http://www3.product-listings.com/index/0140242058
See results from this site only.

next >>

Nine out of 10 relevant hits! All the hits were on target, including an excellent hit (#3) that offers ideas from the National Council of Teachers of English for comparing *Zlata's Diary* to *The Diary of Anne Frank*. Why didn't AltaVista or HotBot lead me to this site? Because they haven't found it yet: Their engines haven't arrived there, or the site didn't notify AltaVista or HotBot yet that it exists. I'm not advocating that Google is better than AltaVista or HotBot. I'm recommending that we need to try more than one search engine every time we search the Web.

One More Search Engine

I also like to use the Northern Light searcher (http://www. northernlight.com). Northern Light boasts of an index of more than 240 million Web pages (#1 ranking in *Nature* magazine's January 2000 study [Butler, 2000; see Figure 3.14, p. 42]).

According to Ji Young Kim at Northern Light, when conducting a search, a site's ranking in a search results list is determined automatically according to a number of criteria, including

➤ Frequency of your search term(s) in the text on the page.

➤ Frequency of the search terms within their entire database of Web sites. (Words that are very common within the entire index will not be assigned as much weight as relatively uncommon words.)

➤ Context of search terms in the page (for example, whether the search terms appear in the title of the page as well as the text).

➤ Natural language analysis of the search terms.

➤ Analysis of the syntax and semantics of natural language queries.

➤ Link popularity (they will also take into consideration how many other sites in their index have links to a page when determining the relevance of that page).

Northern Light also offers a Special Collection of more than 7,000 respected full-text publications, with 25 million pages of business information not otherwise available to Web searchers, such as full-text

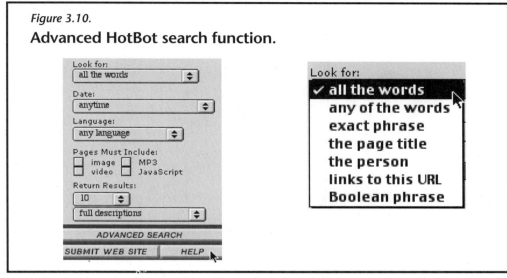

Figure 3.10.
Advanced HotBot search function.

journals, books, magazines, newswires, and reference sources, which are organized into "Custom Search Folders" that you can purchase from them from $1 to $4 per article to be e-mailed to you (http://www.northernlight.com/docs/specoll_help_overview.html).

Many hundreds more search tools are available to educators. Many teachers like the Yahoo directory (http://www.yahoo.com) or the NBCi.com directory (http://www.nbci.com; formerly Snap.com), and search engines Excite (http://www.excite.com), InfoSeek (http://www.go.com), or Lycos (http://www.lycos.com). Later in this chapter (see page 44), we discuss the differences between search engines and search directories.

Another resource is FAST Search's All the Web, All the Time (http://www.alltheweb.com). One of their promotional statements reads:

> According to the latest NEC article in *Nature* magazine, the World Wide Web by mid-1999 contains about 800 million documents, but in our experience with the FAST Web Crawler, over 50% of these are

Figure 3.11.
Google's entry page.

Reprinted with permission of Google, Inc.

duplicates. In May 1999, FAST announced with Dell a catalogue size of 80 million documents. With the current release, over 300 million documents are now searchable, and we will continue to grow with the Web to 1 billion documents and beyond . . . (http://www.alltheweb.com/faq.php3).

The best strategy for teachers is to locate a few search engines and directories that you find most helpful, practice working with them (click on the "Help" button), and become really skilled at using them. Then teach your students.

A Virtual Field Trip for 6th Grade Literature Students

Years ago, when I was first trying out the Web as a resource, I used the Lycos search engine to locate sites about the Mexican holiday, the Day of the Dead. I was teaching my 6th grade literature and writing class the novel *Lupita Manana,* by Patricia Beatty (Beech Tree, 1981), when the kids stumbled over this paragraph in Chapter 12:

> Friday of that week fell on All Souls Day, November 2. An important holiday in Mexico, it was the day when the family dead returned to their homes.

I already knew about *Día de los Muertos,* the Day of the Dead—the annual holiday when families in some Latin America countries celebrate the memories of relatives who have passed away by inviting their spirits back to partake in a family or communal celebration. But none of my 6th graders knew about this holiday, so they were confused. In typical 6th grade fashion, they expressed their opinions and emotions by declaring, "Ooooh, gross!" and "Those people must be sickos!" and "This book is weird!" and "Why don't we ever get to read anything *good*?!" and the ultimate offensive comment: "What time does this period get finished?"

Time to back up and provide them with the knowledge they need to spark their interest: I presearched the Web by going to Lycos and typing in Day of the Dead. Lycos goes right to work hunting across its index, looking for keyword matches: a mere "11,953 relevant results" (Figure 3.15, p. 45).

On checking the first four so-called "relevant results," I was disappointed. Although the 6th graders probably would have been interested in going to hit #3 ("Filth Pig Lyrics"), I wondered *What's going on here? Is Lycos a stupid searcher?* No, at the time I was still an uninformed user.

I neglected to include quotation marks around the four keywords in my search query; Lycos searched for Web sites with "day" and "dead" in them in close proximity. So I tried again, this time making the keywords into a phrase by placing quote marks around them. (Again, remember to use the help features. These search engines *want* you to use their services, so they provide means of helping you navigate through them as best as you can.)

Now that I was searching a *properly constructed key phrase,* rather than a jumble of keywords, I received many relevant results. I selected the best

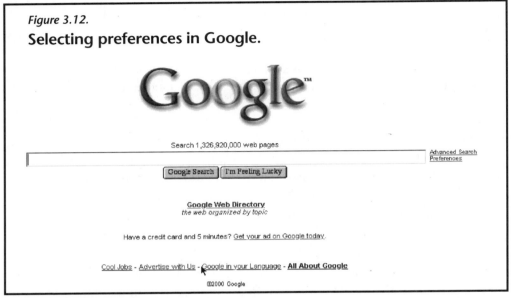

Figure 3.12.
Selecting preferences in Google.

Reprinted with permission of Google, Inc.

four, and the next day I sent my 6th graders to visit those sites on a "virtual field trip," coming up in Chapter 4.

As a sign of how search engines are improving customer service, when I recently tried Lycos again on Day of the Dead, I searched it without quotation marks. The results were surprisingly accurate and a big improvement over a few years ago. Lycos is now programmed to recognize the four words as a popular phrase. Notice that Lycos grouped the four most popular Day of the Dead sites ("Web sites selected based on user selection traffic"); Lycos then followed with many more sites (see Figure 3.16, p. 47).

Searching the Searchers

If you're adventurous and want to see an extensive listing of searchers available on the Web, visit William Cross's "All in One" site (http://www.

> Figure 3.13.
> # Revised Zlata diary search.

Google SM | Zlata diary | 10 results

Search Tips   SafeSearch is Off   Language Options

Zlata's Diary: A Child's Life in Sarajevo
... **Zlata's Diary**: A Child's Life in Sarajevo by **Zlata**...
...03/01/94 **Zlata** Filipovic of Sarajevo began keeping her **diary** in...
members.aol.com/bosfranc/zlata.htm - Show matches (Cache) - 9k - Similar pages

Zlata's Diary Internet Related Resources
... **Zlata's Diary** By Related Internet Resources BosNet ARTICLE - From...
...Resources BosNet ARTICLE - From **Zlata's Diary** The War in Bosnia...
www.arlington.k12.va.us/schools/gunston/teams/special/kschaffner/hiltlang/zlatadia.htm - Show matches

NCTE Teaching Ideas: Building a bridge to The **Diary** of a Young Girl by
...bridge to The **Diary** of a Young Girl by Anne Frank and **Zlata's**...
...classic literature is using **Zlata's Diary** by **Zlata**...
www.ncte.org/teach/Wheeler1161.shtml - Show matches (Cache) - 8k - Similar pages

Zlata's Diary
... **Zlata's Diary** A Review as submitted to a DePaul education class,...
...Review Filipovic, **Zlata**, **Zlata's Diary** Introduction by...
shrike.depaul.edu/~dflapan/zlata.html - Show matches (Cache) - 6k - Similar pages

Zlata's Diary
...Front Page] [Previous] [Next] **ZLATA'S DIARY** by Samatha Zamluk (Age...
...recorded in her **diary**, her whole life changed. **Zlata** was trapped...
www.occdsb.on.ca/~sel/newswave/zlata9.htm - Show matches (Cache) - 4k - Similar pages

Zlata's Diary
... **Zlata's Diary** A Child's Life in Sarajevo With an introduction by...
...Within a couple of months of **Zlata's** first **diary** en- try, Serbian...
www.unc.edu/courses/slav167/zlata.htm - Show matches (Cache) - 101k - Similar pages

zlata's diary
... **Zlata's Diary** This book was about a girl who lived in Yugoslavia...
...see is exactly what **Zlata** describes in her **diary**. I would have...
199.233.193.1/~q4234/br1.html - Show matches (Cache) - 2k - Similar pages

Zlata's Diary - Reader's Program - CUA Orientation
... **Zlata's Diary**: A Child's Life in Sarajevo **Zlata** Filipovic...
...$8.95 ISBN 0140242058 **Zlata's Diary** documents the life, thoughts...
campusprograms.cua.edu/orient/filipov.htm - Show matches (Cache) - 4k - Similar pages

The **Diary** Project
...The **Diary** Project has moved to http://www.diaryproject.com....
www.well.com/user/diary/ - Show matches (Cache) - 4k - Similar pages

Review -- '**Zlata's Diary**: A Child's Life In Sarajevo'
...Review **Zlata's Diary**: A Child's Life In Sarajevo By Tilden...
...book that is a **diary** written by a girl named **Zlata** Filipovic in...
www.igc.org/learn/hgp/aeti-1997/zlatas-diary.html - Show matches (Cache) - 6k - Similar pages

Reprinted with permission of Google, Inc.

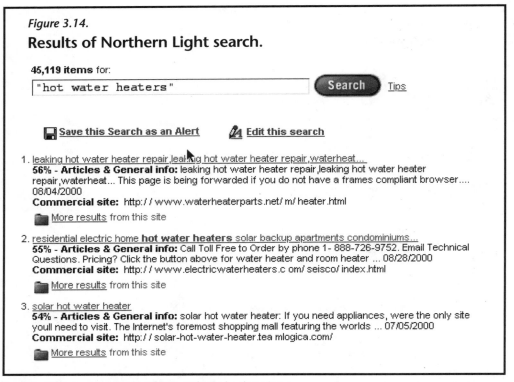

Figure 3.14.
Results of Northern Light search.

45,119 items for:

"hot water heaters"   Search   Tips

💾 **Save this Search as an Alert**   📝 **Edit this search**

1. leaking hot water heater repair,leaking hot water heater repair,waterheat...
   56% - Articles & General info: leaking hot water heater repair,leaking hot water heater
   repair,waterheat... This page is being forwarded if you do not have a frames compliant browser....
   08/04/2000
   Commercial site: http://www.waterheaterparts.net/m/heater.html

   📁 More results from this site

2. residential electric home **hot water heaters** solar backup apartments condominiums...
   55% - Articles & General info: Call Toll Free to Order by phone 1-888-726-9752. Email Technical
   Questions. Pricing? Click the button above for water heater and room heater ... 08/28/2000
   Commercial site: http://www.electricwaterheaters.c om/ seisco/ index.html

   📁 More results from this site

3. solar hot water heater
   54% - Articles & General info: solar hot water heater: If you need appliances, were the only site
   youll need to visit. The Internet's foremost shopping mall featuring the worlds ... 07/05/2000
   Commercial site: http://solar-hot-water-heater.tea mlogica.com/

   📁 More results from this site

Reprinted with permission of Northern Light Technology, Inc.

allonesearch.com), which offers "over 500 of the Internet's best search engines, databases, indexes, and directories in a single site." Or try Scott D. Russell's "Wormhole to the Rest of the Internet" on Oklahoma University's "Explore the Internet" (http://www.wormhole2000.org). He provides a common portal to a variety of the most common search engines, including Metacrawler, HotBot, All the Web, All the Time, AltaVista, Info-Space (reverse telephone lookup), Dogpile, Lycos, Northern Light, Infoseek, WebCrawler, Yahoo, and other search engines, and search tool add-on software. This page also provides a portal for searching for people, computer and Internet (IP lookups, WHOIS) map locations, words (thesaurus, dictionary), weather forecasts, ZIP Codes, sunrise/sunset, parks, businesses, Internet guides and WWW directories, foreign sites, science news, U.S. Government, amateur radio, software, and religious sites. A third site with links to searchers is Locate.com (www.locate.com), which calls itself the "all-in-one search page," with 20 search engines available.

For teachers who say to me, "Just tell me which is the best search engine," the only appropriate and honest answer that anyone can give is, "I don't know." The Web is just too vast and too changing for a single search engine to emerge as the best. Educators need to test the waters by experiencing different searchers to find out for themselves which one(s) help the most.

Search Engine Help Sites

Good news: Help is available from colleagues who have spent a lot of time and energy testing the waters. Their advice and opinions are available (where else?) on their Web sites.

Linda Barlow has created "The Spider's Apprentice: A Helpful Guide to Web Search Engines" (http://www.monash.com/spidap.html), with tips on using search engines like AltaVista, Infoseek, Excite, WebCrawler, Lycos, HotBot, and Yahoo. She writes:

> The Spider's Apprentice, Spidap, is not another search engine. It doesn't crawl the Web looking for new URLs. It can't find stuff for you . . . but it can help you find it yourself. That's what we're all about—helping you search the Web more efficiently. We explain to you how search engines work. We advise you on improving your own search engine ranking by careful use of meta tags and keywords. We guide you in figuring out which search engines are most effective— in fact, we rank them for you (http://www.monash.com/5piap.html).

Other impressive sites include

➤ Debbie Abilock's "Research page" of the library at the Nueva School in the San Francisco Bay Area (http://nuevaschool.org/~debbie/

library/overview). Click on the first link, "Research," then "Choose the Best Engine for Your Purpose" for a nice chart delineating different searchers for different purposes.

➤ Gregg Notess's "Search Engine ShowDown" site, which contains tons of information, including his reviews of the strengths and weaknesses of more than 20 popular searchers (http://www.notess.com/search/reviews).

➤ Ross Tyner's "Sink or Swim: Internet Search Tools & Techniques" in British Columbia (http://www.sci.ouc.bc.ca/libr/connect96/search.htm). He offers us search tips and search engine comparisons (AltaVista, Excite, HotBot, Infoseek, Northern Light), plus some practice exercises.

➤ Terry A. Gray's "How to Search the Web: A Guide to Search Engines" (http://daphne.palomar.edu/TGSEARCH), which states

> Using the various search tools on the Web is enhanced by knowing how they were actually designed, and especially by knowing the specific rules—all too often quite different—for each tool. I have tried to address both these needs. I have arranged the search engines and catalogs in order of usefulness, provided a link to them in the title of each section, and then spell out, in short form, the rules for using them. The goal of this article is to help the new user get the most useful "hits" when using the various tools. At the end I have placed a handy little table that summarizes certain common characteristics among the search engines, some general search tips, and cross-references to other useful articles.

Off to the Web

Just for fun (and for your own education), try a search on "Day of the Dead" or a topic of your own choosing in two or three different search engine databases, and see which one offers the *most* "hits," and which one offers the *best* "hits" on the topic you chose.

Figure 3.15.

First Lycos search for Day of the Dead.

1-10 of 11953 relevant results
Just the links Standard Descriptions Detailed Descriptions

1) Pictures
Every 15 minutes ... Someone in the United States dies in an
alcohol-related traffic collision. Today is the day 24 students at Chico
High School "DIE...
http://www.chs.chico.k12.ca.us/dead.html [100%, 2 of 2 terms]

2) CATECHISM OF THE CATHOLIC CHURCH
CATECHISM OF THE CATHOLIC CHURCH THE PROFESSION OF
FAITH SECTION TWO ARTICLE 11 - "I BELIEVE IN THE
RESURRECTION OF THE BODY" 988 The Christian Creed ...
http://christusrex.org/www1/CDHN/art11.html [92%, 2 of 2 terms]

3) Filth Pig Lyrics
FILTH PIG LYRICS Note from bighair@geocities.com: This is not my
interpretation of the lyrics! Also, this was originally posted on the
Unofficial Mini...
http://www.geocities.com/SunsetStrip/4355/piglyrics.html [88%, 2 of 2
terms]

4) Papyrus of Ani; Egyptian Book of the Dead [Budge]

➤ Danny Sullivan's "Search Engines Tutorials" page on his excellent
"Search Engine Watch" Web site (http://www.searchenginewatch.com/
resources/tutorials.html) provides a comprehensive list of Web sites to
visit for sharpening your Web searching skills. You can also subscribe to
his monthly e-mail newsletter to keep up-to-date on search engine
changes. It is an excellent resource; I have learned more about searching
here than from any other source.

Search Directories

Search engines work electronically, obviously. You type in a keyword or
phrase, and the engine automatically searches its database index looking

for matches. Rather than having human beings standing by to assist you as "online librarians," search engines use software robots, spiders, and crawlers to perform the requested search.

Search directories, on the other hand, have more of a human touch. Anticipating searches such as yours, real, live people look at Web sites and then catalog them into preselected categories, like a library's card catalog. You click on a category that looks the most promising to your search and work your way through the subcategories.

Directories have the advantage of accuracy, because people rather than software are cataloging the sites. You have far less chance of "false hits"—oddball results. But people are slower than software, so directories offer far fewer sites because of the labor required to compile them. The choice is quality versus quantity. At "Search Engine Watch" (http://www. searchenginewatch.com/webmasters/work.html), Danny Sullivan makes the difference clear:

> *Search Engines:* Also called "spiders" or "crawlers," search engines con-stantly visit Web sites on the Internet in order to create catalogs of Web pages. Because they run automatically and index so many Web pages, search engines may often find information not listed in directo-ries. AltaVista is an example of an engine.

> *Directories:* Unlike search engines, directories are created by humans. Sites must be submitted, then they are assigned to an appropriate category or categories. Because of the human role, directories can often provide better results than search engines. Yahoo is an example of a directory.

Yahoo was one of the earliest searchers available on the Internet (the story is that users would be so thrilled at getting help that they'd yell "Yahoo!"); Figure 3.17 (p. 49) is Yahoo's directory (http://www.yahoo. com). When you click on "education," Yahoo presents subdirectories that contain lists of recommended Web sites. Busy Yahoo "librarians" have been previewing sites for users and cataloging them by topic, subtopic, sub-subtopic, and so forth.

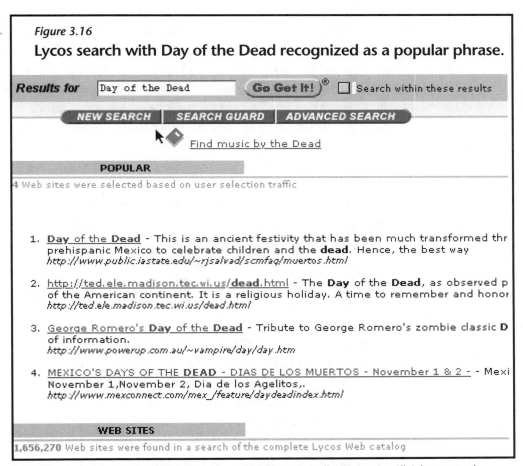

Figure 3.16

Lycos search with Day of the Dead recognized as a popular phrase.

© 2000 Lycos, Inc. Lycos® is a registered trademark of Carnegie Mellon University. All rights reserved.

If you look at the top of Yahoo's home page, you'll notice that above the directory's 14 categories, it also has a search query box, so you can type in your topic to let Yahoo autosearch through its categories for you.

Yahoo also offers "Yahooligans: A Web Guide for Kids" (http://www. yahooligans.com). It works just like Yahoo as a directory, but all cataloged sites have been prescreened for kid-friendliness—that is, their content and presentation are acceptable for students at school.

Another directory worth visiting is "Kidsclick!" created by media specialists in the Ramapo Catskill (New York) Library System for students in grades K–7 (http://www.kidsclick.org) "as a logical step in addressing concerns about the role of public libraries in guiding their young users to valuable and age-appropriate Web sites." Project director Jerry Kuntz reports that as of December 2000, the librarians have examined and cataloged a total of 6,424 Web sites. What's more, the KidsClick! staff double-check the sites every two months to weed out any "broken links" that could cause your students frustration.

I went to KidsClick! to help me find student-appropriate Web sites on Anne Frank for the expanded literature unit with Andy Traisman's 8th graders. Even though KidsClick! targets grades K–7, many of the sites are also appropriate for older students. Instead of clicking through the categories and subcategories, I decided to take the shortcut by typing into the "Search words" field the topic "Anne Frank" (see Figure 3.18, p. 51). Although the KidsClick! librarians had only cataloged two sites, both are excellent. Then I decided to try KidsClick! again, adding +Holocaust to the search. Notice the improvement in choices in Figure 3.19 (p. 52). These offer expanded information relating to Anne Frank.

A third student-friendly directory is Searchopolis (http://www.searchopolis.com), and its more adult-looking layout is excellent for secondary students. High school teachers may also want to check out High School Hub (http://www.highschoolhub.org). Primary teachers may appreciate ALFY (http://www.alfy.com).

We address student search tools and searching techniques in more detail in Chapter 5, "The We Search"; for now, you should understand that when searching the Web, students must "think like librarians." When I ask students what they think I mean by that, though, they stare blankly back at me, probably because the library experience for them while growing up has been so different from what it was for people of pre-Internet generations.

I ask, "If you go the library and ask the librarian/media specialist for information about 'history,' what is the person's response? The answer, of

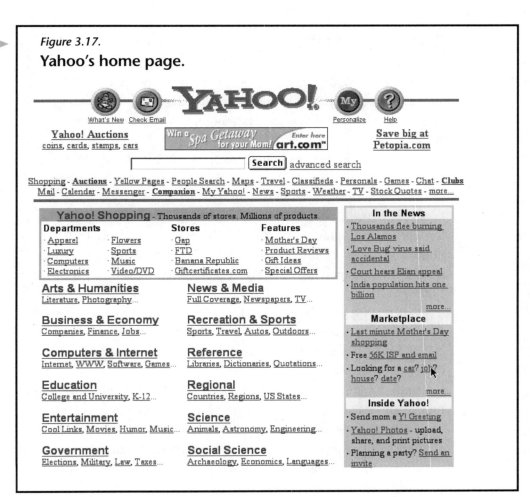

Figure 3.17.
Yahoo's home page.

Reprinted with permission of Yahoo!

course, is, 'Could you be *a little more specific*? Do you need information on U.S. history, or world history, or current events, or what?'"

Everyone who searches the Web must begin to think like librarians and learn to instruct the search engine or search directory to "be a little more specific." One billion-plus Web pages is way too much for any person—or electronic librarian—to handle.

Flashback to Chapter 2

Now is a good opportunity to reflect on using teacher resource Web sites for conducting a Pre-Search. These sites, listed in Chapter 2, pages 11–12, offer directories that link teachers to thousands of sites on common school topics.

Another useful teacher help site is Trackstar (http://trackstar.hprtec. org/). Created by the High Plains Regional Technology in Education Consortium—one of ten regional labs funded by the U.S. Department of Education—TrackStar is a library of teacher-made "tracks" or trails to presearched Web sites on hundreds of topics by grade levels: Early Childhood, Primary (K–2), Intermediate (3–5), Middle (6–8), High School (9–12), College, and Other. See Figure 3.20 (p. 53) to view the TrackStar home page.

When I was presearching for "Day of the Dead," I tried TrackStar to see if another teacher already had done the work for me. I couldn't decide which subject to try, so I used the "Keyword Search" bar and typed in "Day of the Dead."

Sadly, the results came back "0 documents found." But knowing that I must "think like a librarian," I changed my approach to look for the Spanish phrase, *Día de los Muertos*. TrackStar presented me with a track entitled "Día de los Muertos—Espanol I/II." There I found not only a list of sites, but also teacher Heather Olson Beal's notes to her students on what to do while at those sites.

TrackStar also offers its users the opportunity to create their own "Track" of presearched sites, called "Make a Track" (see Figure 3.20). I created a track titled "Internet 3 Key Skills," track no. 13296, which was designed to teach my students how to navigate, comprehend, and evaluate a very clever and funny site called "The Traffic Cone Preservation Site," by UCLA student Amy Winfrey.

Figure 3.18.

KidsClick! search results for Anne Frank.

Search word(s): [ ] [Search] - or, Advanced Search

◉ All fields ○ Web address only

Search subjects by letter: A B C D E F G H I J K L M N O P-Q R S T U-V W X-Z

Search Results

Total Number of Sites Matching Your Search: **2**.

Anne Frank Online - http://www.annefrank.com/
> An online exhibit of Anne Frank and her life and times, produced by the Anne Frank Center USA. Includes information on the Center and the touring exhibit.
> [Illustrations: many | Reading Level: 3-6 | Subject: Holocaust]

Anne Frank - http://www.annefrank.nl/
> Anne Frank was born in 1929 in Frankfurt am Main in Germany. In 1933, the anti-Jewish National Socialist Party led by Hitler comes to power. Anne Frank's Jewish parents Edith and Otto Frank perceive that there is no future in Germany for themselves and their children. They flee to the Netherlands in 1933. Anne is then four years old. In 1940, the Netherlands is occupied by Germany and the protection that Holland provides comes to an end.
> [Illustrations: many | Reading Level: 3-6 | Subject: Holocaust]

Figure 3.19.

KidsClick! search results for Anne Frank and Holocaust.

Search Results

Total Number of Sites Matching Your Search: **10**.

Anne Frank Online - http://www.annefrank.com/
> An online exhibit of Anne Frank and her life and times, produced by the Anne Frank Center USA. Includes information on the Center and the touring exhibit.
> [Illustrations: many I Reading Level: 3-6 I Subject: Holocaust]

Anne Frank - http://www.annefrank.nl/
> Anne Frank was born in 1929 in Frankfurt am Main in Germany. In 1933, the anti-Jewish National Socialist Party led by Hitler comes to power. Anne Frank's Jewish parents Edith and Otto Frank perceive that there is no future in Germany for themselves and their children. They flee to the Netherlands in 1933. Anne is then four years old. In 1940, the Netherlands is occupied by Germany and the protection that Holland provides comes to an end.
> [Illustrations: many I Reading Level: 3-6 I Subject: Holocaust]

C.A.N.D.L.E.S. Holocaust Museum - http://www.candles-museum.com/
> Learn about the historical background to the Holocaust and events of the Holocaust. The C.A.N.D.L.E.S. Holocaust Museum was dedicated in the Spring of 1995. Its purpose is to educate the public about the horrors of the holocaust and to tell the story of the children who survived. Further, visitors learn about the experiments twins were forced to endure.
> [Illustrations: many I Reading Level: 7+ I Subject: Holocaust]

Cybrary of the Holocaust - http://www.remember.org/
> This site deals exclusively with the Holocaust. Included are links to personal interviews with survivors along with other recommended readings and images, so that no one forgets.
> [Illustrations: some I Reading Level: 7+ I Subject: Holocaust]

Holocaust Memorial Center - http://holocaustcenter.org/
> The Holocaust Memorial Center located in metropolitan Detriot offers online exhibits on: Burning of the Books ; Hall of Culture ; Life Chance ; Gates of Auschwitz ; Video Theater ; and Memorial Flame.
> [Illustrations: many I Reading Level: 7+ I Subject: Holocaust]

Holocaust Timeline - http://www.historyplace.com/worldwar2/holocaust/timeline.html
> This site from the History Place features textual information and over 150 photographs.
> [Illustrations: some I Reading Level: 7+ I Subject: Holocaust]

Israel's 50th Anniversary - http://www.worldbook.com/fun/wbla/israel50/html/index.htm
> FIFTY YEARS AGO Israel was born on May 14, 1948, in hope and controversy. Only a few years after the Holocaust, in which 6 million Jews died at Adolf Hitler's hands during World War II (1939-1945), Jewish people worldwide claimed Israel as their own homeland.
> [Illustrations: some I Reading Level: 3-6 I Subject: Israel]

Learning About Lois Lowry - http://www.scils.rutgers.edu/special/kay/lowry.html
> Lois Lowry, author of over 20 novels and winner of the Newbery Medal twice, is a woman to be taken seriously. This native of Hawaii has become a favorite of both children and young adults. She has tackled a number of topics in her literature including adoption, mental illness, cancer, the Holocaust and futuristic societies.
> [Illustrations: no I Reading Level: 3-6 I Subject: Authors, Individual]

The Net's Education Resource Center - http://members.aol.com/aactchrnet/index.html
> This site has links on American History that will help students, parents and teachers access a universe of information from the web. The sites listed are safe for all ages to view. A word of caution on some of the Holocaust material, as it might be too graphic for young kids. If you know where you want to go, just click on the hyperlink below.
> [Illustrations: no I Reading Level: 3-6 I Subject: American History (General)]

Teaching the Holocaust - http://web.macam98.ac.il/~ochayol/kids/einvert.htm
> This teaching unit deals with a major chapter of World War II: the Holocaust. The tasks are carried out through the use of stamps, pictures, children's paintings and text in a computerized virtual environment.
> [Illustrations: many I Reading Level: 3-6 I Subject: Holocaust]

Reprinted with permission of KidsClick!

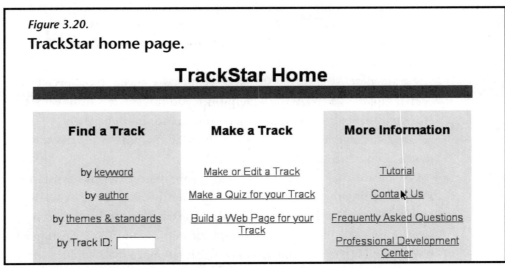

Figure 3.20.
TrackStar home page.

Reprinted with permission of TrackStar/SCR*TEC.

Specialty Search Tools

As educators, we really don't need indexes covering all words on all subjects. As specialists, we can benefit from searchers that focus on educational topics and reduce the volume of possible matches.

For example, math teachers may find the following Math Search tools useful; I found them at Bigchalk's Math site (http://www.bigchalk.com).

➤ Explorer Educational Resources Math Search Engines (http://unite.ukans.edu). Developed jointly by the Great Lakes Collaborative and the University of Kansas UNITE group, the Explorer™ is a collection of educational resources (instructional software, lab activities, lesson plans, student-created materials) for K–12 mathematics and science education.

➤ The Mathematics Archives (http://archives.math.utk.edu). Created at the University of Tennessee Knoxville, this is a multipurpose site for mathematics on the Internet. The focus is on materials that can be used in mathematics education (primarily at the undergraduate level).

Resources available range from shareware and public domain software to electronic proceedings of various conferences, to an extensive collection of annotated links to other mathematical sites.

➤ Leiden University's (the Netherlands) A Collection of Special Search Engines (http://www.leidenuniv.nl/ub/biv/specials.htm#Par51). Hundreds of specialty engines, including #51 for math teachers.

➤ University of Sydney's (Australia) Math Search (http://www. maths.usyd.edu.au:8000/ MathSearch.html).

➤ Swarthmore University's Math Forum offers extensive assistance in the teaching of math, including their "Math Forum Internet Mathematics Library," with links to more than 100 math sites (http://forum. swarthmore.edu/library/resource_types/search_engines). A collection of more than 200,000 documents on English-language mathematics and statistics servers across the Web that is concerned with research-level and university mathematics.

American history teachers may be interested in using Academic Info's "United States History Gateway: Indexes & General Directories" (http:// www.academicinfo.net/histusmeta.html).

World history teachers can benefit from the University of Kansas's WWW-VL History Central Catalogue with sections on "Research Methods and Materials," "Eras and Epochs," "History Topics," and "By Countries and Regions" (http://www.ukans.edu/history/VL/).

HistorySeek! is a directory search engine specifically made for historians, genealogists, scholars, and history enthusiasts (http://www. historyseek.com).

Summary

Learning how to search the World Wide Web is essential to the successful application of the Internet in our schools. Without the ability to narrow this monstrous (and ever-growing) resource to a few helpful sites, users can experience disappointment, mistrust, and even frustrated hostility that could result in turning away from this absolutely amazing tool.

In this chapter, you have learned what search engines are—how they work, where to find "help" tutorials for mastering them, and why you should always use more than one engine. We also learned about search directories—how they work, their strengths and weaknesses. You also were reminded to consult Teacher Help Sites, created by fellow colleagues, that offer links to great educational sites without even needing to conduct a search. You also learned about subject-specific searchers.

Chapter 4 will be a shot of reality. Once you have located the premier sites, what will happen to your students once they arrive there? Will your students actually use these Web sites to learn the new content you're teaching? How many students will have the interest, ability, and fortitude to read the information? How productive will Web assignments prove to be? Chapter 4, "Reading the Web," addresses these critical instructional questions and offers techniques and activities to maximize student learning success on the Web.

REFERENCES

Albert, R. Jeong, H., & Barabasi, A-L. (1999). Internet: Diameter of the World-Wide Web. *Nature*, *401*(6749), 130–131. [Online]. Available by subscription: http://www.nature.com/

Butler, D. (2000, May 11). Souped-up search engines. *Nature*, *405*, 112–115. [Online]. Available: http://www.nature.com/

NEC Research Institute. (1999, August 2). Search engine coverage study published. *The Search Engine Report*. [Online]. Available: http://searchenginewatch.com/sereport/99/08-size.htm

4

READING THE WEB

All the refined Web searches in the world aren't going to help students if they can't understand the material they see when they arrive at those "perfect" Web sites. When comprehension broke down in my 6th grade literature and writing class during study of an assigned novel, I knew I needed to alter my game plan. I had assigned them a "miniperformance task," the mapping/webbing of the plot development for *Lupita Manana*. To reveal early comprehension of the novel's first three chapters, students created electronic graphic organizers using computer software to track the problems that the main characters faced and their solutions to the problems (Lewin & Shoemaker, 1998).*

The breakdown occurred later in the book, with a reference to Mexico's important holiday *Día de los Muertos* (the Day of the Dead). You'll recall from Chapter 3 the students' lack of information about this celebration. Because of this gap in the class's knowledge, their attitude toward the whole book suffered, as did their comprehension. We have all had a similar experience: students who struggle with reading or relating to certain words, concepts, sentences, or paragraphs and therefore experience comprehension meltdown. The challenge is how to overcome these

---

*The material in this chapter originally appeared in a briefer form in Lewin, L. (1999). "Site-Reading" the World Wide Web. *Educational Leadership, 56*(5), 16–20.

obstacles, how to goad the students a little further down the path of comprehension and education, and how to get them to enjoy the ride.

A Virtual Field Trip

The World Wide Web offers a powerful opportunity for teaching better reading. Due to fascination with the Web, students will typically pay more attention to the computer screen than to a teacher lecturing from in front of a blackboard. The key for teachers is to break the students' habitual Web site behavior of click, look, click, listen, click, get the heck outta there to another Web site. Instead, teachers must teach their students how to read the Web—how to "site read." When the incredible expenses of Internet hookup can be used to improve student reading comprehension, the benefits of having the Internet in the classroom spread across the entire learning experience.

To rescue my 6th graders struggling with the Day of the Dead, I deputized the Web to become a crucial element in enhancing their comprehension of the assigned reading. I altered my lesson plan by presearching the Web using Lycos and AltaVista to locate three excellent Web sites that provided students with information (in English) on this holiday. With better appreciation of another culture, they could overcome a major bump in the road to understanding the novel. All the students went to Mexico, Guatemala, and Colombia on a "virtual field trip" to experience this holiday, giving them the benefits of an out-of-school experience without ever leaving the classroom. You might ask, *What made this experience different from reading the material out of a book?* The benefits of the virtual tour include the following:

➤ All the students can look at their own "copy" of the material, while a library might have only one book.

➤ The hyperlink environment provides an enormous number of individual reader options for branching out to related material, compared to the two-dimensional, linear text in a book.

➤ Students have the powerful feeling of control using a computer, versus reading from a traditional source such as a book.

In addition to my Web travels, I employed more traditional resources by checking the card catalog of my school's library, which did have one book on the topic. I wasn't optimistic about the students paying attention to my reading excerpts to the class the next day, nor did I feel enthusiastic about the time needed to photocopy and collate a selected passage for distribution. Of course, I could have tried either or both of the traditional methods: *Just because the Web is available does not mean that traditional resources are to be ignored.* On the contrary, use both the new and the old—whatever works to help teach students is the key.

Even in this modern age, some students are more comfortable with material they can hold in their hands, and perhaps some auditory learners in your classrooms would benefit from hearing the material, rather than being subjected to the many distractions that often accompany a Web experience. As with any educational tool, the test of success is: Do students actually *understand* the information provided, by whatever medium? Some do; some might; some are very unlikely to. That's the reality of instruction in any classroom.

Reading for Understanding with the "E-Sheet"

The reality of classrooms today, and in the future, is that the Internet is going to be a central part of their learning experience. Just as students need to comprehend material that they read on paper or hear from an instructor, they need to know how to comprehend information delivered electronically. A reading comprehension device that can assist them is the electronic worksheet, or "E-Sheet" (see Figure 4.1). The E-Sheet helps students focus on reading comprehension by asking them to answer a set of guided questions provided to them in a word processing file saved onto their floppy disks. For my students researching the Day of the Dead, as they read the information at the three preselected Web sites, they toggled back to the word processor to type in answers. Back and forth they went: from the Web to the E-Sheet, from the browser to the word processor, multitasking, reading and writing, reading and writing. Not one student complained: They actually liked it! As their teacher, I liked it, too, because they were actually learning the content information I was teaching. They were engaged, and the repetitive nature of the task helped reinforce the material.

That this E-Sheet provides students with more than one Web site to visit is not unintentional. Why offer several sites when one site might have been sufficient? Because you should be prepared for the Internet to sabotage your lesson plans. On its best days, the Internet is quirky. Web sites move or are eliminated, periodically go down for updating, are sometimes slow loading . . . something can always happen to foul up an activity. But don't let this possibility keep you from using the Net. After all, you wouldn't stop using a library because a book is checked out, but you *would* make sure that a certain book is at the library before uprooting your whole class to look at it. Because the availability of a particular piece of information on the Internet is never 100 percent assured, having options is always the best plan—so list multiple sites on an E-Sheet for students. If one site is causing problems, the others may come to the rescue.

Another tip for using E-Sheets: Before sending a class to the computers for an E-Sheet assignment, have them count off by the number of sites. If you have three sites for students to look at, divide the class into groups of three. Students in group 1 go to site 1, students in group 2 go to site 2, etc. By breaking the students into user groups in this manner, you reduce traffic flow to each site, which means that the sites will "load" more quickly.

A Goal of Comprehension

The purpose of tools such as the E-Sheet is to make the most of students' reading time. Comprehension continues to be a key goal of our nation's

Figure 4.1.
Sample E-Sheet #1.

Guided Reading: Electronic Worksheet
E-Sheet for Día de los Muertos

KIDPROJ   **All Soul's Day**

http://www.kidlink.org/KIDPROJ/MCC/11.1.2.html

1. Who wrote this entry?
2. What country is she from?
3. How do they celebrate this holiday?
4. What does "fiambre" mean?

EXTRA CREDIT:

5. What are some other holidays celebrated there? (HINT: click on **"country"** button.)

The Day of the Dead

http://www.dayofthedead.com/
1. Who wrote this entry?
2. Find her picture. What is your estimate of her age?
3. What other pictures do you find?
   a.
   b.
   c.
4. Click on Chapter Three of her book: What photograph do you see?

EXTRA CREDIT:

5. Copy and paste the photograph here:

schools. New technologies have not diminished our students' need to read. In fact, the arrival of computers and the Internet in the classroom *increases* the importance of reading comprehension. Every school district knows this.

For example, in Oregon where I teach, the Department of Education has developed a set of Learner Performance Standards that all students need to meet (Oregon Department of Education, 1997). The Standards expect students to be able to

➤ Use a variety of reading strategies to increase comprehension and learning.

➤ Demonstrate literal, inferential, and evaluative comprehension of a variety of printed materials.

➤ Connect reading selections to other texts, experiences, issues, and events.

Other states also recognize the critical necessity of reading. Delaware's (2001) Grade 5 Performance Indicators for English/Language Arts list

➤ 13 indicators to "Demonstrate an Overall Understanding of Printed (and Oral) Texts."

➤ 9 indicators to "Critically Analyze and Evaluate Information."

➤ 3 indicators to "Self-Monitor Comprehension."

Washington's State Commission on Student Learning (State of Washington, 1998) lists three strands in its Essential Academic Learning Requirements for both "Reading for Literary Experience" and "Reading to Learn New Information, to Perform Tasks, and for Career Applications." Students are expected to

➤ Comprehend important ideas and details.

➤ Analyze, interpret, and synthesize.

➤ Think critically.

Check your state and district's expectations for students' ability to read with comprehension. The extensive list you will undoubtedly find reflects the critical importance that reading holds for student success in school and beyond. So, how can the Web help us?

Chris Birch, a teacher at Saeger Middle School in St. Charles, Missouri, presearched the Web and found some great sites to help him instruct his class about the Salem Witch Trials of the 1690s. To ensure that his students would actually read the information at those Web sites, he designed an E-Sheet on his word processor, Microsoft Word (see Figure 4.2).

As you can see, creating E-Sheets is easy. In your word processor, type three things:

➤ The names of the Web sites.
➤ The sites' addresses (remember that accuracy is essential when keying in URLs).
➤ The set of guided questions for each site.

E-Sheets are useful for everyone from elementary teachers to high school teachers. They also apply to any subject area. To view an E-Sheet online, see the "Teaching with the Internet" site (http://www.teleport.com/ ~llewin/inbound/site_reading/site_reading.html).

Primary teachers, of course, may need to adapt the E-Sheet for younger readers. Instead of each student receiving an E-Sheet for individual work on the Web, children in grades K–2 could work collectively on an E-Sheet projected from the teacher's computer to a white screen in the front of the room. Students give answers orally for the teacher to type onto the E-Sheet. (For details, see Option 3 under "The One-Computer Classroom," p. 68.)

Enhancing the E-Sheet Experience

As helpful as E-Sheets can be, managing them can be cumbersome. First, having scores or even hundreds of students each day save their E-Sheet files onto floppy disks is time-consuming. Instead, teachers can save their E-Sheet files onto the school's file server computer, so that many students

Figure 4.2.
The Salem Witch Trials Electronic Worksheet.

Christopher Birch
Saeger Middle School • St. Charles, MO

1. (http://www.salemwaxmuseum.com/twitch.htm)
   What were the beliefs of witchcraft? (There are five)

2. (http://www.salemwitchmuseum.com)
   Who was the first to be tried and was she found guilty or innocent?

3. (http://www.ogram.org/17thc/andover_petition.shtml)
   What five women was the petition written for?

4. How many people signed the petition?

5. (http://www.salemweb.com/memorial/default.htm)
   Name the five women tried and condemned on June 29-30.

6. (http://www.rci.rutgers.edu/~jup/witches/salem.html)
   Give the dates and how each died for the following people:
   -Rebecca Nurse
   -John Proctor
   -Giles Corey
   -Martha Corey

7. (http://www.salemweb.com/tourism/witchhouse/default.htm)
   The Salem Witch House was once the home of who?

8. (http://school.discovery.com/schoolstore/videos/rediscovering
   america-thesalemwitchtrials/vocab.html)
   Define scapegoat.

9. (http://www.salemwitchmuseum.com)
   Copy the picture on this website and place it on your worksheet.

Reprinted with permission of Christopher Birch, Saeger Middle School, St. Charles, MO.

can access them simultaneously and rapidly from any computer that is connected to the school's network. If you don't know how to do this, you can ask the technology coordinator for your school. Ask that person to create a directory (folder) on the file server with your name on it, and place the E-Sheet file—saved as a *template*—in there for your students. A template is an electronic document that is simultaneously accessible to multiple users; it allows them to type in and save their own individual answers.

While you have the tech person's attention, why not create another directory entitled "Student Work," so students can save their finished E-Sheets there instead of onto floppies? The advantage of this approach is the speed of opening E-Sheet files from the file server rather than popping 50, 60, 125 floppies in and out of your computer's floppy drive. The disadvantage of placing material on your school's network is that multiple student access to a "public" directory of saved student work runs the risk of sabotage. As Sean Rill, technology coordinator for the Susquehanna Township (Pennsylvania) School District, suggests, discuss with your technology coordinator options for preventing student tampering of another's work. One possibility is to have students save their completed E-Sheets in both places: onto the file server computer for you and onto their floppy as a backup. (The necessity of backups is another important lesson for students, although—as for everyone else—this lesson is often best learned the hard way.) Another option is to set up password-protected student "save" folders on the school's file server, which students can access only with passwords they have selected. (Again, your school's technology coordinator can help you here.)

Another way to enhance the E-Sheet experience is to go beyond answering text-based questions to incorporate pictures onto the E-Sheet, as Chris Birch's class did (see question 9 in Figure 4.2). Copying a picture from a Web site and pasting it onto an E-Sheet is easy; both Netscape Navigator and Internet Explorer have this capacity.

For PC users of Netscape, find the image you want, use the mouse to place the cursor over the image, and click and hold the right button. A window opens up with a number of choices. Select [Save image as] and save it to an appropriate file on your C (or other) drive or to a floppy disk (see Figure 4.3). Finally, open it into your word processor or other software, such as PowerPoint.

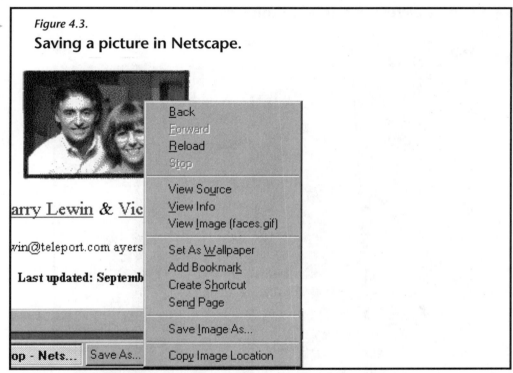

Figure 4.3.
Saving a picture in Netscape.

Netscape Communicator browser window © 1999 Netscape Communications Corporation. Used with permission. Netscape Communications has not authorized, sponsored, endorsed, or approved this publication and is not responsible for its content.

The Mac version of Netscape is even easier. Click on the desired image and a pop-up menu appears. [Copy this image], multitask back to the word processor where the E-Sheet is, and [paste] the image wherever you want it.

Both Mac and PC versions of Explorer follow the simple [copy] and [paste] technique described for the Mac version of Netscape (see Figure 4.4). (PC users, remember to use the *right* mouse button.)

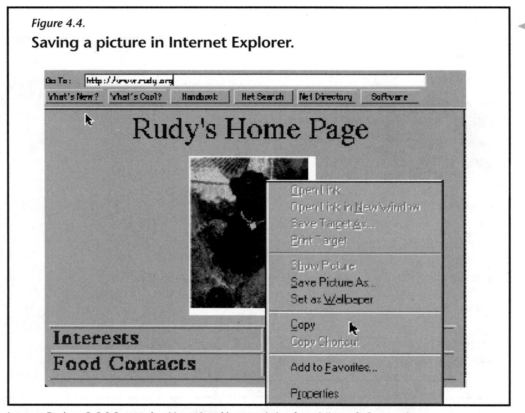

Figure 4.4.
Saving a picture in Internet Explorer.

Internet Explorer® 5.0 Screen shot(s) reprinted by permission from Microsoft Corporation.

A third modification to an E-Sheet can guide students beyond literal questions. Instead of merely asking students to recall and retype information, stimulate their thinking by asking upper-level questions, such as interpretations, compare and contrasts, evaluations, analyses, and critiques.

The One-Computer Classroom

E-Sheets work well for individual students working on their own assigned computers in the school's lab. But what if your school doesn't have a computer lab because the machines are distributed to the classrooms? Or what if there is a lab, but you have no access to it because it's used all day for computer classes? What if the lab is available for sign-up, but your insensitive colleagues don't understand that you should have first rights to it whenever you want, and you end up out of luck?

If you have a one- (or two- or three-) computer classroom, you can still assign E-Sheets for your students. Here are some options for incorporating the presearched Web into your curriculum in your classroom.

Option 1: Rotate individual students, or pairs of students, to the computer for a finite amount of time. Of course, class sizes being what they are in many schools, this time allotment may need to be brief, so E-Sheets must be short enough for students to complete quickly. An alternative is to assign a full-length E-Sheet collectively to the class. Each student (or pair) answers one (or two) questions, then rotates off for the next student(s) to find the Web site answer to the next question(s). Students then share their answers, which provides a nice combination of group and individual learning. Remember to post a sign-in sheet near the computer(s), so you can later recall when and by whom the computer was used.

Though this approach may not be ideal, most of us don't teach in an ideal setting. Although it would be wonderful for every school district to provide every student, teacher, administrator, and staff member with a laptop computer and a wireless Internet connection, that's just not in everyone's immediate future. So teachers need to do the best with the resources that are available, just as we have always done.

Option 2: Connect your single classroom computer to a TV monitor for whole-class viewing. Some newer computers and TVs are pre-wired to be able to "talk to each other." Sadly, many computers and TVs-on-a-cart aren't on speaking terms, but an intermediary device allows computer images to be "read" and presented on a TV monitor. Known as *scan converters,* these little boxes (price: $80–$300) make whole-class presentations possible. Many brands are available on the market, with varying degrees of clarity. The TV monitor is large enough for everyone to see, so all students in the class can contribute to completing a communal E-Sheet displayed on the TV. As an alternative, each student can receive a hardcopy of the E-Sheet (now a worksheet) to fill in with a pencil as the answers are found on the TV-presented Web sites. One caveat is that some scan converters' quality is subpar for effective classroom use. So, whatever brand your tech coordinator buys, try to obtain a trial offer in case you're not satisfied with the images.

Also, with a scan converter you will have to enlarge the text of the Web browser so students in the back of the room can see it. Most browsers default to 12-point font, which is too small for classroom use. Netscape for Windows offers font enlargement under [Preferences], as indicated in Figure 4.5. Mac users of Netscape find similar instructions. Internet Explorer 5.0 for PCs has located the [Fonts] command under the [View] menu (Figure 4.6, p. 70). In Internet Explorer 5.0 for the Mac, the [Fonts] command is under the [Edit] menu's [Preferences].

Option 3: Use an LCD panel on top of your overhead projector to project the site's image from the computer onto a large white pull-down screen in front of your classroom. Teachers who already use this technology know its drawback: The overhead's bulb isn't always powerful enough to project a bright image to the big screen, so the classroom lights need turning off. Also, as the LCD panel heats up during the viewing period, the image tends to become wavy and somewhat distorted.

A far better (though more expensive) option is for your school to purchase a computer multimedia projector. These projection devices have very powerful bulbs that project big, bright images to a white screen. With a multimedia projector, teachers don't need to dim the classroom lights. Prices vary from about $1,500 to $12,000, and the quality goes up with the price. Ask your technology coordinator or tech team to look into

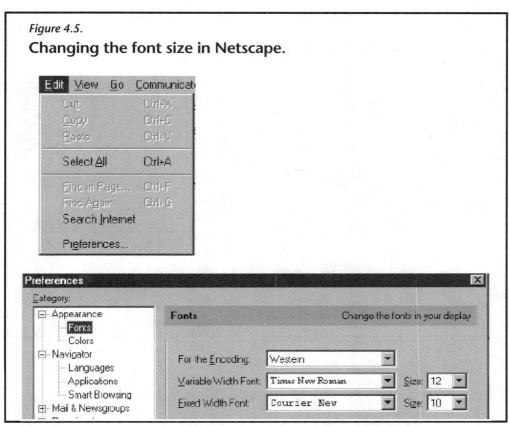

Figure 4.5.

Changing the font size in Netscape.

Netscape Communicator browser window © 1999 Netscape Communications Corporation. Used with permission. Netscape Communications has not authorized, sponsored, endorsed, or approved this publication and is not responsible for its content.

this option. Naturally, to justify the expense, you'll probably need to share this equipment on a cart with other teachers.

Reading for Deeper Meaning

E-Sheets are great for forcing careful reading, but they mainly assist the first level of reading comprehension: literal understanding of the basic facts presented by the author. Many teachers want their students to

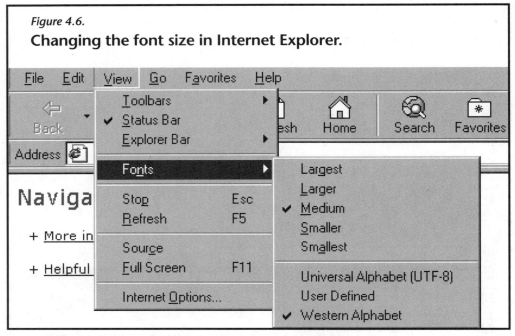

Figure 4.6.
Changing the font size in Internet Explorer.

Internet Explorer® 5.0 Screen shot(s) reprinted by permission from Microsoft Corporation.

operate on a deeper level of understanding. The challenge is to extend student's learning beyond the text to relate it to some other source or experience—to synthesize the author's information with additional information from another book, article, Web site, movie, TV show, or personal experience. That is, students must connect other information to the assigned Web reading. This next level of comprehension is a challenge for most students.

For example, my 8th grade language arts/U.S. history class was studying the Boston Massacre of 1770. They read for comprehension from their history textbook, but when asked to connect the textbook's account of this historical event to some other source, they stumbled. Most students had no other prior source of information. (That is, they couldn't recall any information from previous history courses.) So, I went to the Web. How many Web sites do you think exist on the topic of the "Boston Massacre"?

Plenty, including the excellent "From Revolution to Reconstruction" by George Welling at the University of Groningen in the Netherlands (http://odur.let.rug.nl/~usa/), introduced in Chapter 1. He has posted more than 100 primary source documents on U.S. history. I assigned the 8th graders to read two of the entries: Captain Thomas Preston's account (the British commanding officer) and an anonymous eyewitness account (from a Bostonian). Not surprisingly, these accounts reflect widely different points of view. Not only were the students expected to read each account for understanding, but they also were expected to compare and contrast them.

The beauty of the Web for this assignment was its ability to bring far-flung resources right into the school for our students.

Reformatting Web Sites for Improved Readability

As the old saying goes, with the perks come the quirks. Sometimes when Web sites are text-intensive, as Welling's site is, the design and format of the site makes reading the information on it difficult and uninviting. Take a look at Figure 4.7, which is the second page of Capt. Thomas Preston's gripping court testimony. The long paragraph and the small print, not to mention the tough vocabulary, will challenge a student historians' ability to comprehend the important information the captain is providing.

When reviewing sites for classroom use, the literally countless numbers of Web pages come in four categories:

➤ Perfect Web sites for what we are studying: excellent information presented in an interesting format. Teachers and students are always happy to find that perfect Web site.

➤ A subset of the first category: Perfect Web sites for what the class is studying, but the information is presented in ways that are difficult to comprehend.

➤ Other Web sites that are fine but have nothing to do with what we're studying. In the interest of time, teachers and students both need to discipline themselves not to become bogged down looking at these types of sites.

➤ Sicko Web sites (racist, sexist, violent, pornographic) created by nut cases. Teachers of course must prescreen these out of view of the students, and perhaps the school system has filters built into their Web access that keep these sites out of the school building. (Chapter 5 goes into more details on filters.)

Figure 4.7.

A hard-to-read Web site excerpt.

On Monday night about 8 o'clock two soldiers were attacked and beat. But the party of the townspeople in order to carry matters to the utmost length, broke into two meeting houses and rang the alarm bells, which I supposed was for fire as usual, but was soon undeceived. About 9 some of the guard came to and informed me the town inhabitants were assembling to attack the troops, and that the bells were ringing as the signal for that purpose and not for fire, and the beacon intended to be fired to bring in the distant people of the country. This, as I was captain of the day, occasioned my repairing immediately to the main guard. In my way there I saw the people in great commotion, and heard them use the most cruel and horrid threats against the troops. In a few minutes after I reached the guard, about 100 people passed it and went towards the custom house where the king's money is lodged. they immediately surrounded the sentry posted there, and with clubs and other weapons threatened to execute their vengeance on him. I was soon informed by a townsman their intention was to carry off the soldier from his post and probably murder him. On which I desired him to return for further intelligence, and he soon came back and assured me he heard the mobb declare they would murder him. This I feared might be a preclude to their plundering the king's chest. I immediately sent a non-commissioned officer and 12 men to protect both the sentry and the king's money, and very soon followed myself to prevent, if possible, all disorder, fearing lest the officer and soldiers, by the insults and provocations of the rioters, should be thrown off their guard and commit some rash act. They soon rushed through the people, and by charging their bayonets in half-circles, kept them at a little distance. Nay, so far was I from intending the death of any person that I suffered the troops to go to the spot where the unhappy affair took place without any loading in their pieces; nor did I ever give orders for loading them. This remiss conduct in me perhaps merits censure; yet it is evidence, resulting from the nature of things, which is the best and surest that can be offered, that my intention was not to act offensively, but the contrary part, and that not without completion.

Source: "From Revolution to Reconstruction: An Html Project" http://odur.let.rug.nl/~usa/D/17511775/ bostonmassacre/prest.htm Used with permission.

Many Web sites are in the second category. For example, a person, company, or organization creates a fine Web site on a topic of interest, but doesn't have the elementary or secondary school audience in mind. Maybe the vocabulary is challenging, or the format is confusing, or the information comes in huge paragraphs, or, as in this case, the material is presented in its original form: as testimony from over 200 years ago.

Just because these Web sites appear difficult at first glance does not mean they are unusable. Teachers can reformat them to improve readability and thus enhance student reading comprehension. Modifying electronic text and images from the Web becomes easy with practice. For example, a new, improved version of Capt. Preston's testimony appears in Figure 4.8.

How did I reformat material from the Web site? I simply borrowed parts of Preston's testimony from the Web site and placed them into a word processing document, using the following procedure:

1. At the Web site, use the cursor to highlight the words you want.
2. Select [Edit] and [copy].
3. Go to your word processing program.
4. Create a [new] document.
5. Select [Edit], and [paste] the information in the new document.

Once you have the text in your word processor, you can reformat it any way you want. To improve the readability for my history/language arts class, I changed the font, added paragraph breaks, typed in a few definitions to key words, and posed guided questions.

Using the reformatted document, students had an easier time reading for comprehension. Once they understand assigned material at a deeper level, they can go beyond the text and relate it to information gleaned from other sources, one of the primary criteria for demonstrating reading proficiency.

Notice at the bottom of Figure 4.8 that I provided a citation of my source material. Students should always see their teachers giving appropriate credit for material that they did not create. Proper citations of

Figure 4.8.
A Web site reformatted for ease of instruction.

Boston "Massacre" Testimony of British Capt. Thomas Preston

On Monday night about 8 o'clock two soldiers were attacked and beaten.
Significance?

But the party of the townspeople in order to carry matters to the utmost length, broke into two meeting houses an range the alarm bells, which I supposed was for fire as usual, but was soon undeceived.
Translation:

About 9 some of the guard came to and informed me the town inhabitants were assembling to attack the troops, that the bells were ringing as the signal for that purpose and not for fire, and the beacon (bright light) intended to be fired to bring in the distant people of the country. This, as I was captain of the day, occasioned my repairing (moving) immediately to the main guard. In my way there I saw the people in great commotion, and heard them use the most cruel and horrid threats against the troops.
Significance?

In a few minutes after I reached the guard, about 100 people passed it and went towards the custom house where the king's money is lodged. They immediately surrounded the sentry posed there.
Translation:

and with clubs and other weapons threatened to execute their vengeance on him. I was soon informed by a townsman their intention was to carry off the soldier from his post and probably murder him.
Reliable Source?

Source: "From Revolution to Reconstruction: An Html Project" http://odur.let.rug.nl/~usa/D/17511775/ bostonmassacre/prest.htm Used with permission.

Figure 4.8—continued.

A Web site reformatted for ease of instruction.

Boston "Massacre" Testimony of British Capt. Thomas Preston

On which I desired him to return for further intelligence, and he soon came back and assured me he heard the mobb (old spelling for mob) declare they would murder him.
Significance?

This I feared might be a preclude to their plundering (stealing) the king's chest. I immediately sent a non-commissioned officer and 12 men to protect both the sentry and the king's money, and very soon followed myself prevent, if possible, all disorder, fearing lest the officer and soldiers, by the insults and provocations of the rioters, should be thrown off their guard and commit some rash act.
Translation:

They soon rushed through the people, and by charing their bayonets in half-circles, kept them at a little distance. Nay, so far was I from intending the death of any person that I suffered. The troops go to the spot where the unhappy affair took place without any loading in their pieces;
Translation:

nor did I ever give orders for loading them. This remiss conduct in me perhaps merits censure;
Do you agree?

yet it is evidence, resulting from the nature of things, which is the best and surest that can be offered, that my intention was not to act offensively, but the contrary part, and . . .

Source: "From Revolution to Reconstruction: An Html Project" http://odur.let.rug.nl/~usa/D/17511775/ bostonmassacre/prest.htm Used with permission.

borrowed or reprinted material are crucial to good scholarship, and with the Internet, the possibility of plagiarism is obvious when students can simply cut and paste long sections of text into their work. Model "giving credit where credit is due" for your students. And if the Web site states something like, "All material here is copyrighted and requires permission to use in any form," e-mail the site's webmaster, asking permission to reformat it for your students.

Of course, a clever teacher in grades 4–12 could eventually assign students to work in pairs to create their own versions of a reformatted Web site. This task would really force young Web readers to read for deeper meaning because in order to rewrite and reformat information, one must truly understand it. Add some big-time motivation: Make the assignment into a contest. Honor the best reformatted site by using it during the next term or next year with your new class. Of course, you would credit the budding webmasters with a proper citation.

"Translating" a Web Site

An alternative strategy to the Web readability issue is to assign to the students not just a reformatting of the Web material, but a translation of the site into language that their peers can understand better. Instruct students to visit a presearched Web site, but caution them that while the information at the site is useful to the topic being studied, the site's webmaster needs a little help in improving the readability for students. To make the assignment flow more smoothly, the teacher must decide in advance which sections of the Web site to assign to particular students, how long to make the sections for translation, whether students work in pairs or independently, and how much time to allot for this task.

Teachers can approach the translation assignment in two different ways. The first option is for students to receive a printed section of the

Web site. On this hardcopy, which the teacher creates by [copying] text off the site, [pasting] it into the word processor, and triple-spacing it, students use colored pencils to write the meaning of the text in their own words between the lines. With the second option, students visit the site "live" on the Web, [copy] their assigned section, [paste] it into the word processor, and edit it as a word processing document.

The second option has advantages for teachers who want to familiarize their students with working with the Web and feeling comfortable and confident at the keyboard. Students generally have more fun multitasking between the Web browser and the word processor, and experiencing the ease of electronic editing as opposed to working on hardcopy. The disadvantages to electronic editing in the classroom are as follows: more time required on the computers—that is, competition to sign up for them—and teaching students the cut-and-paste trick (some already know it, others don't). Also, many teachers would rather avoid cutting and pasting from Web sites in hopes of discouraging the "digital plagiarism" temptation, which we discussed briefly in this chapter and which we address in more detail in Chapter 6.

The translation activity is a good beginning for training students in a critical researching skill: how to paraphrase while avoiding plagiarism. One excellent Web site that you can send students to is "Bats" (see Figure 4.9). This site, created by Cy Young at Jaguar's Paw Resort in Belize, has short, easy-to-read paragraphs in white text on a dark background. But even so, it still needs some rewriting for elementary-level comprehension. Send the students there, and give them the task of writing it in their own words.

The ability to translate also is effective when students are taught the We Search, which we discuss in detail in Chapter 5. The We Search requires students to search for, and then *carefully read*, Web sites on an assigned topic.

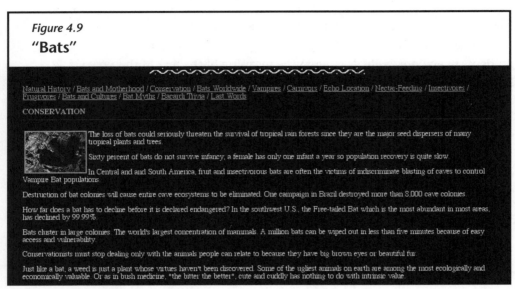

Figure 4.9
"Bats"

Natural History / Bats and Motherhood / Conservation / Bats Worldwide / Vampires / Carnivors / Echo Location / Nectar-Feeding / Insectivores / Frugivores / Bats and Cultures / Bat Myths / Bacardi Trivia / Last Words

CONSERVATION

The loss of bats could seriously threaten the survival of tropical rain forests since they are the major seed dispersers of many tropical plants and trees.

Sixty percent of bats do not survive infancy; a female has only one infant a year so population recovery is quite slow.

In Central and and South America, fruit and insectivorous bats are often the victims of indiscriminate blasting of caves to control Vampire Bat populations.

Destruction of bat colonies will cause entire cave ecosystems to be eliminated. One campaign in Brazil destroyed more than 8,000 cave colonies.

How far does a bat has to decline before it is declared endangered? In the southwest U.S., the Free-tailed Bat which is the most abundant in most areas, has declined by 99.99%.

Bats cluster in large colonies. The world's largest concentration of mammals. A million bats can be wiped out in less than five minutes because of easy access and vulnerability.

Conservationists must stop dealing only with the animals people can relate to because they have big brown eyes or beautiful fur.

Just like a bat, a weed is just a plant whose virtues haven't been discovered. Some of the ugliest animals on earth are among the most ecologically and economically valuable. Or as in bush medicine, "the bitter the better", cute and cuddly has nothing to do with intrinsic value.

Reprinted by permission of Cy Young.

Critiquing a Reading

A third indicator of reading competence is the ability to read critically with an eye toward analyzing content. Young readers performing this task must "take a critical stance, standing apart from the text, to make supported judgments." Students demonstrate successful performance of this task by "suggesting more than one interpretation, challenging the author's assumptions, or providing feedback to the author on what could have been included, omitted, or changed" (http://www.ode.state.or.us/asmt/resource/scorguides/rd41201.pdf). This indicator of prowess sounds pretty tough, doesn't it? How does a teacher move a student to this demanding level? One way is to deputize the Web.

For example, in studying Colonial American history, my students learned about the arrival of the English colonists in North America and the impact of their presence on Native American tribes. We focused on Jamestown Colony and the Powhatan tribe, which are famous due, in part, to Pocahontas and Capt. John Smith. As part of my instruction of this key historical event, my class compared and contrasted Disney's *Pocahontas* to textbook accounts, to primary source documents, and to a biography of Pocahontas (*The Double Life of Pocahontas*, by Jean Fritz, Puffin Books, 1983). Additionally, I directed the students to two Web sites that provided further information:

➤ The Walt Disney Studios at that time had some background information on the film.

➤ The Powhatan Renape Tribe presented Chief Roy Crazy Horse's open letter criticizing the Disney Studios' version of the Pocahontas story (http://www.powhatan.org/pocc.html).

Naturally, I expected my students to be keen *readers* of the content information and to be skillful *comparers* of multiple sources. To help them in this task, I created an E-Sheet to guide their visits to these sites. I also wanted them to become *critical analyzers* of the texts, so they composed letters about their reactions to the Disney version and Chief Roy Crazy Horse's opinion in his open letter. The students, as was the task of the instruction, were able to (1) interpret the facts in more than one manner, (2) challenge the assumption of either author by providing an alternate viewpoint, and (3) offer feedback to the author on what material could have been added, changed, or omitted. By using the Internet, the students could locate and analyze the alternate viewpoints they needed to complete the task.

A final assignment requires students to write a historical persuasive letter, in which young historians write convincingly about their analysis of a historical event (Lewin and Shoemaker, 1998). Through the school's online access, the students were further able to leverage their use of Internet technology by e-mailing their letters to either Disney in Anaheim or the Powhatan Renape Tribe in New Jersey. Even without e-mailing the results, the assignment is a motivating, engaging one. If a school does not offer students e-mail accounts, and students still want to send their historical persuasive letters via more traditional methods, then they can type their letters into a word processor, edit them (remembering to spell check *and* proofread them, since spell checkers are not infallible), print them, and mail them in an envelope.

With instructional time being so valuable, a modification to this lengthy letter writing assignment could be to write a memo instead of a letter. Students love writing memos, mainly because memo-writing is a new experience for most of them; memos are short, and students love the "TO:, FROM:, RE:" format. Tana's memo to the author of her history textbook, critiquing a chapter on what happened to Columbus's first settlement, appears in Figure 4.10.

Figure 4.10.

A student's memo to a textbook writer.

TO: Ernest R. May
From: Tana _____
Date: September 30, 1997
RE: Proud Nation, p. 35

I think the story in your textbook "Christmas Day, 1492" is well written. I liked the part about it "being God's will" that the Santa Maria sank.

It is short, but you didn't leave out a lot of detail.

You could have added what, exactly, happened to Columbus's Fort La Navidad. I want to know who burned it down, who killed the men, and I want to know why they did it.

Alternatively, students can use the word processor to create a post-card (an "E-Card") to send to you, the textbook author, the author of a novel, a webmaster, or a classmate (see Figure 4.11).

Summary

The primary goal of all educators is to improve students' academic performance, and no academic skill affects more areas of intellectual pursuit than reading. Throughout time, teachers have used any resource available that can help in this important endeavor. The World Wide Web is such a resource, especially because of its engaging appeal to students of all grade levels and varying abilities. By encouraging "site reading" and using the variety of tools that the Internet provides, teachers can help students improve their reading performance, both on and off the Net.

Web site visits in the schools should ensure and enhance learning, not just assign bouts of unproductive "surfing" that let students become accustomed to using computers. Many students are already doing that at home. E-Sheets, reformatting sites, translating sites, e-mailing letters of critique, and writing memos and postcards are all ways of making the classroom experience more productive. All these benefits can emerge from teachers working with presearched Web sites.

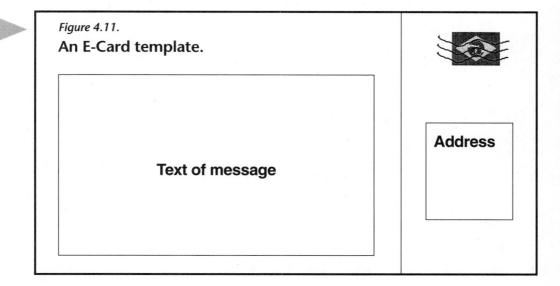

Figure 4.11.
An E-Card template.

Text of message

Address

But what about releasing students to Level 2, the We Search? The next chapter moves students up to this more independent level of Web use.

REFERENCES

Delaware Department of Education. (2001). Grade 5 Performance Indicators for English/Language Arts (http://www.doe.state.de.us/standards/english/ELA_Standards.html).

Lewin, L. (1999). "Site-Reading" the World Wide Web. *Educational Leadership, 56*(5), 16–20.

Lewin, L., & Shoemaker, B. J. (1998). *Great Performances: Creating Classroom-Based Assessment Tasks.* Alexandria, VA: Association for Supervision and Curriculum Development.

Oregon Department of Education. (1997). Learner Performance Standards (http://www.ode.state.or.us/cifs/standards/cimtabloid-2000.pdf).

State of Washington. (1998). Essential Academic Learning Requirements (http://www.k12.wa.us/reform/EALR/standards/read.asp).

5

The We Search: Intermediate Student Use of the Web

After repeated experiences with the first level of Internet activity, the Pre-Search, students eventually will become ready for more independent use of the Web. I call this second level the We Search.

As introduced in Chapter 2, in the We Search the teacher determines the topic of study but then releases all the students to search the Web to find sites that inform the class on the topic. At this point, the students need to know how to conduct their own searches to locate appropriate sites on a given topic or area of study.

The classroom instructor decides when the students are ready to go to this level. Some classes—for example, at the middle school or junior high school level—may not be ready for the We Search because of immature behavior and the accompanying lack of trust on the part of the instructor. In the early elementary grades, taking on Web searching may not be developmentally appropriate; the teacher makes this decision.

Web Searching: The Agony Before the Ecstasy

Conducting Web searches, as we teachers know from our own experience, is not always easy. Even after years of practice, we all still face the frustration of attempting to use a search engine to narrow the field of Web sites down from over 1 billion pages to a few useful ones, only to receive lists of hundreds of recommended sites, many of which don't even remotely match our search query. We also have learned firsthand that even seemingly legitimate searches return inappropriate results, with perfectly innocent requests for material revealing sites dedicated to all types of wacko, sexist, racist, violent, or pornographic tendencies. It's surprisingly easy for this to occur.

As teachers, we certainly fear that our students could have the same experience. They, too, can face too many sites and an accidental (or purposeful) arrival at an inappropriate Web location. But with the progress of time and the growth of the Web comes good news. Some Web search tools—search engines and search directories—are increasingly designed to address both of these concerns. When accessing the Internet's World Wide Web, remember that its popular usage is barely 10 years old, and with technology so young, growth sometimes outpaces quality, especially in a field that is essentially uncontrolled. As time goes on, search tools will increasingly accommodate user needs and demands, both for more information and occasionally less. Until that time (and nothing—not even the Internet—is ever entirely foolproof), teachers need to limit the access that students have, much in the same manner that active parents do for their children.

Controlling the Flow: Tools That Limit Student Web Access

When a teacher decides to move students to Level 2, the students essentially have free access to the Web. Students at this stage conduct their own searches to locate sites related to the assigned topic. Let's look at search tools and other software that try to prevent both an overload of sites and arrivals at objectionable sites.

Directories

As you'll recall from Chapter 3, with directories, human beings prescreen
Web sites. These librarians of the electronic world actually visit Web sites,
check them out, and read through them before recommending them to
student searchers. Any site reviewed and placed in a directory designed
for student education surely won't be trashy. With directories, students
generally find fewer sites to choose from, but they're receiving quality
over quantity.

For younger students (elementary and middle grades, ages 7 to 12)
Yahooligans (http://www.yahooligans.com) garners rave reviews. Created
by Yahoo, this "Web Guide for Kids" offers prescreened sites on thousands of topics. When a young Web searcher conducts a search at Yahooligans, no inappropriate sites will show up—only those deemed readable,
reliable, appropriate, and generally useful for educational purposes for
students at this age. Additionally, Yahooligans, as shown in Figure 5.1,
offers a search shortcut: type key word(s) into the search box above the
directory's six general categories, and Yahooligans will automatically
search through its directory for you.

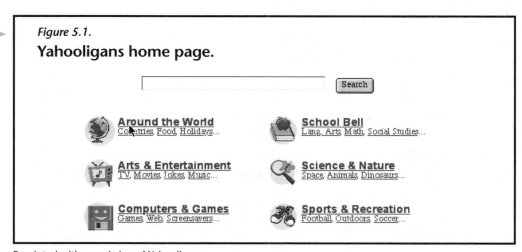

Figure 5.1.

Yahooligans home page.

Reprinted with permission of Yahooligans.

KidsClick! (http://www.kidsclick.org) is another recommended student directory. KidsClick! checks its sites every two months to ensure that they are still active and available, removing some 200 dead sites after each review. This feature is particularly helpful, because we want to limit discouraging attempts to find information. Students should be made to feel that accessing the World Wide Web is an inviting experience, not one filled with disappointments. Teachers, too, can feel invited by employing Yahooligans and KidsClick! themselves during a Pre-Search. I had success with KidsClick! on Anne Frank (refer to Chapter 3).

Another kid-friendly search tool is Ask Jeeves for Kids (http://www.ajkids.com). Editors—working for "Jeeves," the helpful butler—place preselected sites in a "knowledgebase" (questions with answers). Additionally, the metasearch engine in Ask Jeeves for Kids connects to Yahooligans and Education World, which also contain sites that are hand-picked by editors. Jeeves describes his site:

> Each Web site included in Ask Jeeves for Kids is carefully selected by an editor. We include only "G-rated" pages and those written specifically for children. We select sites for the quality and depth of their content, and for safety.

Secondary teachers should consider assigning Searchopolis (http://searchopolis.com/). Like Yahooligans and KidsClick!, Searchopolis is a directory, and its current categories are humanities, social sciences, languages, history, science, and math, plus over a dozen reference sources. Searchopolis also offers the search shortcut box, as well as a search choice of preselected Web sites or an online encyclopedia, Encarta. It also has "readability" software designed to match resources with reading levels. Figure 5.2 shows the opening screen for Searchopolis. Early elementary teachers should visit ALFY, "The Web Portal for Kids" (http://www.alfy.com/teachers/teach/alfys_library/index.asp). Click on the "Teachers" link to "Thematic Unity," "Lesson Plans," or "ALFY's Library." I must say, though, that these links load very slowly, at least on my computer.

Figure 5.2.
Searchopolis opening screen.

Reprinted with permission of Searchopolis.

Three other options for a safe We Search are Education-World (http://www.education-world.com), which is loaded with educationally appropriate sites; AOL NetFind Kids Only (http://www.aol.com/netfind/kids); and the Lycos search engine, which also offers a set of resources for students (geography, history, language arts, math, reading, science, plus additional references of a kids' almanac, encyclopedia, dictionary, and an atlas) in its KidsZone (http://www.lycoszone.lycos.com/homework.html). Writing in *Educational Technology* (1999), Lilla, Hipps, and Corman report their findings on "Academic Subject Directories." By analyzing directories for authority, content, and navigation/graphics, they rank their top five:

> ➤ Britannica Internet Guide (http://www.britannica.com)
> ➤ StudyWeb (http://www.studyweb.com)
> ➤ BUBL LINK (http://bubl.ac.uk/link)
> ➤ INFOMINE (http://infomine.ucr.edu)
> ➤ The Internet Scout Project (http://scout.cs.wise.edu)

Filters

The second type of search tool that prevents access to inappropriate sites runs software programs that block sites containing objectionable words. Words deemed pornographic, violent, or profane are stored in a database.

When a student attempts to enter a site (either accidentally or on purpose) containing one of these stored words, the software blocks it—that is, "filters" it out.

For example, AltaVista offers the "Family Filter" option (see Figure 3.1 on page 21), and Google now has added a new feature, "SafeSearch," to filter adult content out of its listings by preventing sites with pornography or adult content from appearing in Google's listings. To activate the SafeSearch feature in Google, first do a search, then select the Preference link that appears on the top of the results page. Go down to "SafeSearch Filtering" and select it. Any future searches will then be filtered. Google states, "While no filter is 100% accurate, Google's filter uses advanced proprietary technology that checks keywords and phrases, URLs and Open Directory categories for more than 200 million web pages" (http://www.google.com/intl/en_extra/help/customize.html#safe).

Danny Sullivan at Search Engine Watch lists more sites with filtering options:

➤ Alta Vista's Family Filter (http://www.altavista.com)
➤ Lycos SearchGuard (http://searchguard.lycas.com/)
➤ CleanSearch.com (http://www.cleansearch.com)

More About Web Blocking Software

Many software products are also available to screen inappropriate sites from appearing on your school's computers. The Sutter County (California) School District offers a link (http://www.sutter.k12.ca.us/security/blocking/block.htm) to the following filtering programs:

➤ CyberPatrol
➤ Times Up
➤ Library Safe
➤ NetNanny
➤ Net Cop
➤ SurfWatch

➤ Xstop
➤ WEB Sense

"Ask Jeeves" recommends these filtering programs:

➤ SurfWatch
➤ CYBERSitter
➤ CyberPatrol

Jeeves links to them from his site (http://www.ajkids.com/dearPare.asp).

The generic term for blocking the arrival of some Web sites onto a system is "establishing a firewall." Teachers can feel more confident releasing their students to perform a We Search knowing that screening help and firewalls are available. The bad news is that filtering software is not foolproof. Some potentially offensive sites still slip through cracks in the wall. How? By avoiding the use of obvious words that screening software tries to find. Software is not infallible; it's just software, as prone to errors and oversights as are the humans who write it. A pornographic site without profanity or explicit descriptions could slip through the firewall, as can pornographic pictures.

Likewise, firewall software can be overindustrious and end up blocking perfectly appropriate sites accidentally. The most often used example of an overzealous screener is one that treats "breast" as an offensive word, thus keeping a student from conducting a search for information on breast cancer. Another example came from a high school literature teacher in a workshop I presented, who told the group, "When I did a search on *Macbeth*, I got zero results. When I checked with my district's network guy, he told me the sites were blocked because they contain the word *damn* (Lady Macbeth's famous speech, 'Out, damned spot. . . .')"

So, firewalls are not 100 percent effective. However, some school districts still like having the help, so they install a firewall on their network. Network administrators can also customize firewalls by typing in the address of Web sites known to be inappropriate. Alternatively, network administrators can release improperly or inadvertently blocked sites.

Asking Questions

One search tool simplifies the We Search by allowing users to ask questions instead of creating search queries. Ask Jeeves for Kids is one student-friendly site: instead of typing in key words to activate the search engine, the student uses "natural language" by merely typing in a question followed by a question mark and clicking on "ask." Jeeves's software culls out the key words and sends the query to two search directories, Yahooligans and Education World, to conduct the search. The results come back quite quickly and usually accurately (see Figure 5.3).

AltaVista, which is one of the most popular general-use search tools, also offers searching by typing in a question.

Figure 5.3.

An example of a natural language search tool, Ask Jeeves for Kids!

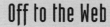

Off to the Web

Teachers or students can compare performing a search to asking a question. Go to AltaVista (http://www.altavista.com) and try a key word(s) search; then try asking a question to determine which approach is more successful for you. Remember, though, that the results of this comparison can differ depending on the particular topic requested and the words that you include in your question. For example, I first tried a search query: +"Larry Lewin" +Rudy to locate Web sites that have both me and my dog, Rudy. Notice that I correctly placed "+" signs immediately before *both* terms (with a blank space before the second sign) and put quotes around my name (to make it a phrase), as instructed by AltaVista's "Help" button. (See Chapter 3 under "Dealing with Search Results.")

The search results saddened me: Only one site on the entire World Wide Web contained both terms—my own site. But then I typed a question into AltaVista's "Search for" bar: Where can I learn information about Larry Lewin and his dog Rudy?

Amazing! 31,658,248 pages found! But they all were "false hits"— none actually had information about the pup and me. The first hit: Kurt Lewin, the famous social psychologist. The second hit: Rudy's Alaska Fishing and Snowmobiling Page. (As far as I know, the dog hasn't yet been to Alaska to fish or snowmobile, and he isn't even mentioned at Kurt's site.)

So in this example, learning how to type proper search queries (with quote marks and "+" and "-" signs) was far more accurate than typing in a question. For young searchers, however, question-asking may prove to be a nice entré into learning how to search the Web with engines.

Monitoring Student Web Use

During a We Search, a class of students could be allowed to use search engines, although some teachers prefer using only search directories with students at this level. But if you have a class whose Internet use you feel confident about, search engines of course can be helpful. Even teachers who have the greatest confidence in their students' Web use need to monitor the activity and just remain alert for possible abuses of this resource—not that all students are waiting for the opportunity to sneak into a chat room, a porno page, or the official Starlet-of-the-Day Web site. In fact, probably only a handful of potential misusers are in any classroom.

First, all schools need to write an Acceptable Use Policy (AUP) for the Internet. Every member of the school community—students, teachers, administrators, and parents—must understand the school's rules and expectations about Internet use. An AUP states the do's and don'ts of Internet usage on school property and requires signatures of agreement from students and parents/guardians. Nancy Willard at the University of Oregon has created an AUP that she calls a "Responsible Netizen Model Internet Use Policy" (see Figure 5.4).

If your school does not yet have an AUP in place, check out the following sites for ideas:

➤ http://www.4j.lane.edu/4jnet/4jnetstudentapp.html
➤ http://connectedteacher.classroom.com/tips/aup.asp
➤ http://www.itrc.ucf.edu/WORKSHOPS/Telecom2/
AUP_template.html

Once students and parents sign the AUP contract, students are responsible for honoring it, but teachers still need to monitor Internet usage to ensure fulfillment of the contract. Consider the four following monitoring methods.

Figure 5.4.

An Acceptable Use Policy (AUP) for the Internet.

Responsible Netizen
Model Internet Use Policy

Nancy Willard, Project Director
Center for Advanced Technology in Education
College of Education, 5412 University of Oregon
Eugene, Oregon 97403-5412
541-326-3460 (office) 541-346-2565 (FAX)
E-mail: nwillard@oregon.uoregon.edu
URL: http://netizen.uoregon.edu

A.   Educational Purpose

XYZ District's Internet system, XYZNet, has a limited educational purpose. Activities that are acceptable on XYZNet include classroom activities, career development, and high-quality personal research. You may not use XYZNet for entertainment purposes (, except for those periods of time that the school has designated as "open access".) XYZNet is not a public access service or a public forum. XYZ District has the right to place reasonable restrictions on the material you access or post through the system. You are expected to follow the rules set forth in XYZ District's disciplinary code and the law in your use of XYZNet. You may not use for commercial purposes. This means you may not offer, provide, or purchase products or services through XYZNet. You may use the system to communicate with elected representatives and to express your opinion on political issues, but not for political lobbying.

B.   Student Internet Access

The Web is a global database system providing access to information from around the world. Students may have access to Internet Web information resources through their classroom, library, or school computer lab.

E-mail is an electronic mail system, which allows students to communicate one-to-one with people throughout the world. Elementary students may have e-mail access only under their teacher's direct supervision using a classroom account. Elementary students may be provided with individual e-mail accounts under special circumstances, at the request of their teacher and with the approval of their parent. Secondary students may obtain an individual e-mail account with the approval of their parent. You and your parent must sign an Account Agreement to be granted an individual e-mail account on XYZNet. This Agreement must be renewed on an annual basis. You parent can withdraw their approval at any time. Students may not establish web e-mail accounts through the XYZNet.

If approved by your principal, you may create a personal web page on XYZNet. All material placed on your web page must be preapproved. Material placed on your web page must relate to your school and career preparation activities.

Reprinted with permission of Center for Advanced Technology in Education, College of Education, University of Oregon.

Self-Monitoring

The first approach to monitoring Internet use is student self-monitoring. Students who are inadvertently sent to an inappropriate Web site from a search can act as self-blockers by refusing to stay there. Students who arrive at a Web site that falls outside AUP parameters have a decision to make, and their choice can be the smart one or the not-so-smart one. The smart choice is to "just say no," click the "Back" button in Netscape or Explorer to back out of the site (see Figure 5.5), and perhaps even notify the teacher or technology coordinator of the offensive URL in order to block the site from future access. The not-so-smart choice is to pump a fist, yell "Allllright!!" and call over a few buddies to check out the goodies. Of course, the student making the latter choice faces consequences that are spelled out in the signed AUP contract.

Figure 5.5.
The "Back" command in Netscape.

Netscape Communicator browser window © 1999 Netscape Communications Corporation. Used with permission. Netscape Communications has not authorized, sponsored, endorsed, or approved this publication and is not responsible for its content.

Occasionally a student strays into an offensive site and wisely tries to exit it by clicking the "Back" button, only to be led deeper into the trash. Devious site programmers know how to manipulate Web site movement in this manner, with a technique known as "mousetrapping." In such a case, a student has three good options from which to choose. Notify the teacher; click on the "Home" button in the browser program (Netscape or Explorer), which routes them to a home Web site selected by the technology coordinator (usually the district's or school's home page); or restart the browser for a fresh start.

"Go" and "History"

A second method of monitoring student use of the Internet is to use the "Go" and "History" functions. Both major Web browsers, Netscape and Explorer, have these built-in tracking devices. They allow the user to "go" back to any previously visited site simply by clicking on "Go" and releasing on the desired site. They also serve as monitors.

For the "Go" function, a teacher simply stops at a student's computer and asks the student to click on the "Go" command to unveil a trail of sites recently visited. Figure 5.6 shows one result of such a "Go" check performed on a 7th grader using Netscape for Mac.

The good news is that the student visited excellent search tools: Magellan, Ask Jeeves for Kids, Lycos' KidZone, and Northern Light. The bad news is that just before the "Go" check, he was trolling at the "Spice Girls Nude" site—needless to say, not an assigned part of the We Search.

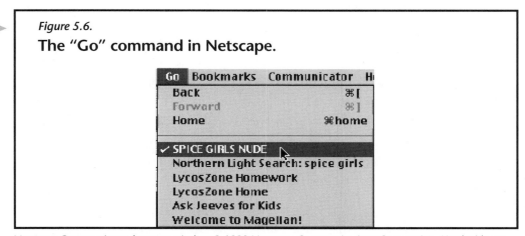

Figure 5.6.
The "Go" command in Netscape.

Netscape Communicator browser window © 1999 Netscape Communications Corporation. Used with permission. Netscape Communications has not authorized, sponsored, endorsed, or approved this publication and is not responsible for its content.

The student was busted three times for violating the school's Acceptable Use Policy: first for visiting a site not related to the assigned topic; second for visiting an off-limits, inappropriate site; and third, for obvious bad taste in music. The punishment was an example of tough technological love: loss of Internet rights for two weeks (not to mention whatever additional home consequences might have been levied).

For a school that is using a particular ISP (Internet Service Provider), other ways to perform the "Go" check may be to click the down arrow in the box that displays the current URL.

For more complete information than the "Go" command provides, a teacher with Netscape access can require a student to click on the [Communicator] menu at the top, select [Tools], and go across to [History]. This command reveals not only the names of the recently visited sites, but also their addresses. A teacher who thinks any site might be suspicious can tell the student to click on it, and Netscape reroutes back there. The shortcut with a Mac platform is to type the [Apple+H] keys. For Windows users of Netscape, see Figure 5.7 on how to access the "Go" and the "History"; notice the keystroke shortcut for "History" is [Ctrl+H].

Internet Explorer, the other popular Web browser, also allows a teacher to track a student's trail. Instruct the student to click on the History menu at the top. A window opens with a folder of Today's sites, as well as sites from past days and weeks (see Figure 5.8, p. 98).

Internet Explorer for Mac users (see Figures 5.9 and 5.10, pp. 99 and 100) click on a past day's date to arrive at a window showing where a student was on that particular day at that particular time. Explorer saves this data onto the hard drive (the "C" drive on PCs), so the history is retrievable even after Explorer has been [Quit] or [Closed].

Hard-Drive Monitoring

A third way to monitor student Web use employs behind-the-scenes recordkeeping that stores Web visit information on the "C" drive (in

Windows) or the hard drive (in Macs). Netscape calls this the "Global History," and Explorer names it "History." This function keeps a file of all Web sites and Web images viewed on that particular computer. (A teacher may receive quite an education by reviewing this file every so often.) With this function in Netscape, a teacher can check up on a student after the fact by returning to his or her computer and typing in *about:global* (see Figure 5.11, p. 102). Netscape will access all the Web sites and all the images on those sites and list them. When the sites (ending in .html) and images (ending in .gif or .jpg) are listed, sadly they are not in chronological order. So, to locate a certain day, I click on [Edit] and select [Find (on this page)] and type in the desired date, such as Feb. 9. Netscape jumps right to that date. To jump to the next Feb. 9 site, select [Find again]. (See Figure 6.5 in Chapter 6.)

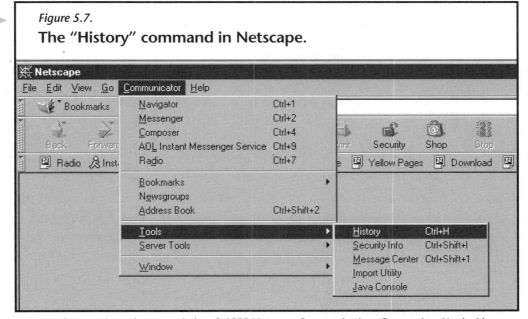

Figure 5.7.

The "History" command in Netscape.

Netscape Communicator browser window © 1999 Netscape Communications Corporation. Used with permission. Netscape Communications has not authorized, sponsored, endorsed, or approved this publication and is not responsible for its content.

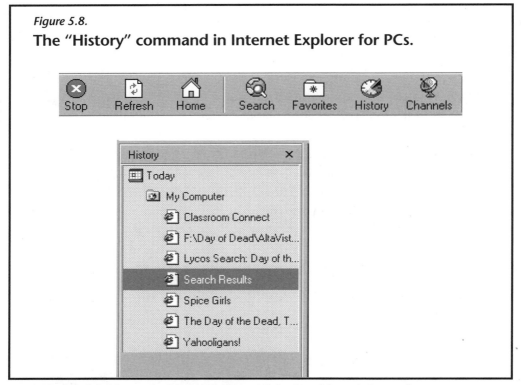

Figure 5.8.

The "History" command in Internet Explorer for PCs.

Internet Explorer® 5.0 Screen shot(s) reprinted by permission from Microsoft Corporation.

For Internet Explorer, doing a history check is simple. Explorer allows us to set the History to "live" on the C drive (or Mac hard drive) for as long as we want it to—even after the student has Quit, Closed, or Exited the program. On a PC, click on the menu option [View] and select [Internet Options]. In the "History" box, click on the up or down arrow to set the number of days you want Explorer to keep track of visited sites in the "History" window. With a Mac, click on the menu option [Edit] and select [Preferences]. Select [Advanced] and then click in the "History" box to set the numbered or remembered sites.

Using the "History" monitoring method is best done after students have left the room, so that those who don't already know about this

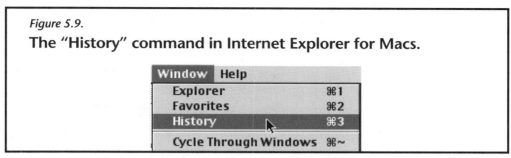

Figure 5.9.

The "History" command in Internet Explorer for Macs.

Internet Explorer® 5.0 Screen shot(s) reprinted by permission from Microsoft Corporation.

feature don't find out. If kids discover the "History" function, they may soon discover that they can trash or recycle these files, thereby removing incriminating data. Of course, knowing which student used which computer on what day and at what exact time is essential to making sure that any problems are traced to the correct student. For this reason, keeping a seating chart for the computer lab or sign-in log in your classroom is a crucial aspect of Internet monitoring.

Trashing or recycling "History" files is an action that you or the technology coordinator should perform on your computers periodically anyway. By deleting these old files, you reclaim room on your hard drive. As soon as you restart Netscape or Explorer, a new list begins.

External Monitoring Software

A fourth way to monitor students is to purchase off-the-shelf software that allows school personnel to track students' activity on the Internet. Perhaps your school's or district's technology coordinator knows about these products or can investigate their purchase and use.

Mac users should consider Apple's Network Assistant, which allows a teacher or computer lab instructor to observe individual students' computers from the teacher's computer. Imagine being able to see from your own desk what any student in the room is doing at their own computer (http://www.apple.com/education/k12/networking/appleshareip/ana/)! PC users have a choice of software packages for monitoring:

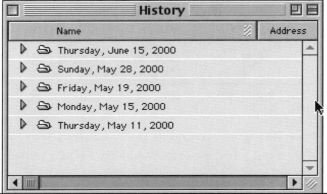

Figure 5.10.
A day-by-day "history" retrieved in Internet Explorer for Macs.

Internet Explorer® 5.0 Screen shot(s) reprinted by permission from Microsoft Corporation.

➤ CyberSnoop (http://www.pearlsw.com/school/gim.html)
➤ NetOpSchool (http://www.crossteccorp.com/netopschool/index.html)
➤ LANSchool (http://www.lanschool.com)

Once students find out that their teachers can observe them from a central computer, mischievous behaviors typically cease immediately—i.e., the "chill factor" kicks in.

More "Traditional" Electronic Resources for a We Search

Back in Chapter 1, you learned (or were reminded) that the World Wide Web is only one part of the Internet . . . a very exciting part, but not the only one. Many excellent student and teacher Internet resources on countless topics don't come from Web pages posted by individuals. Rather, students can perform their We Search at online library sites that offer more traditional sources, such as encyclopedias, book chapters, magazine articles, and other documents.

Libraries

Like real libraries, many online libraries require a library card, for which schools or school districts would pay a subscription fee. The cost to schools depends on the size of the school and the number of concurrent users for which the school wishes to obtain access. One such fee-based service is Electric Library (http://www.elibrary.com) by InfoNautics, which offers over five million online full-text documents and image items in the following categories: magazines, maps, books and reports, newspapers and newswires, radio, TV and government transcripts, and pictures.

Some libraries offer free online resources:

➤ *Awesome Library* (http://www.awesomelibrary.org) "organizes the Web with 15,000 carefully reviewed resources, including the top 5 percent in education." Last year it averaged 1.5 million "hits" or 350,000 page views per month and was ranked by Links2Go as 37th in popularity globally on the Internet (Yahoo was number one). Created by The Evaluation and Development Institute (EDI), which was formed to promote world peace by the year 2050, Awesome Library offers links to materials in the arts, English, mathematics, science, social studies, health and physical education, technology, and languages.

➤ *The U.S. Library of Congress* (http://www.loc.gov) Web site is the Internet location of the largest library in the world, home to an enormous number and variety of collections. Comprised of approximately 115 million items in virtually all formats, languages, and subjects, these collections are the single most comprehensive accumulation of human expression ever assembled. True to the Jeffersonian ideal, the collections are broad in scope, including research materials in more than 450 languages, over 35 scripts, and in many media. Of course, not all Library of Congress materials are available electronically, but its Web site still is home to many publications, links, and exhibitions.

➤ *The Internet Public Library* (http://www.ipl.org) is a wonderful resource for a variety of collections, some directed specifically to teens and youth. Their published mission is to "serve the public by finding, evaluating, selecting, organizing, describing, and creating quality information resources, (and to) develop and provide services for our community with an awareness of the different needs of young people."

➤ Library Spot (http://www.libraryspot.com). This site describes itself as "a free virtual library resource center for educators and students, librarians and their patrons, families, businesses and just about anyone exploring the Web for valuable research information." It has links to libraries online, film libraries, government libraries, image libraries, medical libraries, and presidential libraries.

Figure 5.11.

The "about:global" command in Netscape for Windows and Macs.

Netscape® Windows

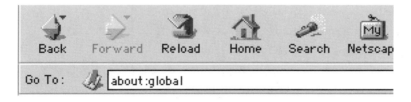

Netscape® Mac

➤ *Information Please* (http://www.infoplease.com). This resource offers online almanacs, encyclopedias, and dictionaries (links under "Sources"). Claiming to be "all the knowledge you need," Information Please has international and U.S. facts, as well as directories of information on people, society, science and technology, sports, business, and economics, as well as Web site reviews.

Encyclopedias

Rather than going through search directories, search engines, and other forms of linkages, students can gain direct access to several free online encyclopedias:

➤ *ElectricLibrary's Encyclopedia.com* (http://www.encyclopedia.com) has more than 14,000 free articles from *The Concise Columbia Electronic Encyclopedia* (3rd ed.).

➤ *Britannica.com* (http://www.britannica.com) describes itself as a "free knowledge and learning center for people who seek thoughtful and engaging context to today's affairs. Only Britannica.com lets users simultaneously search the world's most respected encyclopedia, expert reviews of the Web's best sites, timely articles from leading magazines, and related books." This Web site comes from the *Encyclopedia Britannica* group, which began publishing in 1768.

➤ *Encyclopedia Smithsonian* (http://www.si.edu/resource/faq) is another huge, free resource to teachers and students. It is loaded with thousands of sources on hundreds of topics.

As useful as online resources may be, the same cautions apply to them as apply to any other Web site. Just as we warn our students about the dangers of blindly accepting information off a Web site as being true, accurate, credible, or reliable, students also need to understand that just because information is disseminated by a seemingly reputable source does not automatically mean that the information is accurate. Traditional school resources, such as encyclopedias and books, need to be scrutinized as well. They can contain factual errors, and by omission they can misrepresent reality. As always, the best methods for research involve consulting with multiple sources that represent a variety of viewpoints. In our final chapter, we address the source credibility issue further by teaching our students how to become critical consumers, as opposed to passive absorbers, of digitized information. Such discretion is especially important when they go to Level 3 of Internet use, the Free Search.

REFERENCE

Lilla, R., Hipps, N., & Corman, B. (1999, November/December). Searching for the yahoos: Academic subject directories on the Web. *Educational Technology, 39*(6), 33–39.

6

THE FREE SEARCH: INDEPENDENT STUDENT USE OF THE WEB

Many students with Internet access at home attempt to convince their teachers that both the Pre-Search and the We Search are unnecessary because they already possess advanced Internet skills due to "years of Internet surfing" at home. Don't be fooled.

What can we presume about students' use of the Internet at home? What do they use it for in the evening after dinner? How about chat, e-mail, and visiting Web sites of their favorite sports teams or musical groups? Home use of the Net is typically for entertainment purposes, which is fine as long as their parents approve. But in school, the Internet is not an entertainment medium; we use it for educational purposes. Therefore, the teacher is the person to determine if and when students are released to this third level of Internet use: the Free Search, which allows them to select a topic of their choice (related to the course or class and approved by the teacher) and then conduct independent research on the Web.

The determination of when students are proficient enough to embark on the Free Search depends on students' proficiency at the Pre-Search and the We Search levels. Once they've demonstrated skills and responsibility in these areas, it's time to consider moving them on to the Free Search.

Independent searches require specific student skills for success. Students need to know how to

➤ Prepare for a search.
➤ Employ search engines and directories.
➤ Evaluate the content accuracy at Web sites.
➤ Record information from their selected sites.

Let's first consider preparation strategies to set them off in the right direction.

Prepare for the Free Search

As with any educational activity, students experience a higher degree of success when they precede the activity with some mental preparation. Teachers know that the prewriting stage of the writing process is critical for student authors, because without time devoted to thinking, planning, and brainstorming, many young writers will flounder. Science teachers also know about advance preparation for a lab experiment; turning the class loose in a science lab without advance preparation is asking for failure and potential trouble. Social studies teachers never send their students to the school library to conduct research without first spending quality time planning it out. Otherwise, students arrive at the library clueless about how to proceed and alienating the media specialist, who is an important ally. Regardless of the subject matter or activity, preparation is always essential.

The same principle holds true for Free Search of the Internet. Students need to prepare before heading out on the Web for a search of self-selected topics. Preparation can take a variety of forms. Among them are the graphic organizer and the K–W–L sheet.

Graphic Organizers

One way to have students prepare for an Internet Free Search is to assign a preparatory graphic organizer. First introduced in Chapter 4, a graphic organizer such as a concept map or diagram can help students organize their thoughts before searching the Web.

For example, after conducting a Pre-Search on Mexico's Day of the Dead holiday and sending my class to the preselected sites, students expressed so much interest in this topic that I released them to Level 2 for a We Search. Knowing that they needed to prepare, I assigned them to create a graphic organizer with three sections: (1) what we already knew about this holiday (from our Pre-Search), (2) what additional information we could find about it (including history, cemeteries, and altars), and (3) translation of the holiday's name into Spanish. This 20-minute exercise paid off, as demonstrated by Clare's graphic organizer in Figure 6.1. Notice that she used graphics software—in this case, Inspiration® Software—to create a design that differentiated the assignment (the diamonds) from the material that completed the assignment (the circles).

Preparation for a Free Search also benefits from graphic organization. In a U.S. history class, Ben requested the research topic of "U.S. Law." At first, I was a bit skeptical. When I asked Ben about his interest in this particular topic, he replied, "Because my mom is an attorney, and my dad is an attorney, and guess what I want to be if I get into a good law school?" Given his reasons, and that we were studying the U.S. Constitution, Ben was granted approval for his Free Search topic. He created an electronic graphic organizer using available software, which he presented in great detail (see Figure 6.2, p. 109), following a modified K–W–L approach.

K–W–L Sheets

Another method of preparing for a Free Search involves a more low-tech, though no less effective, method: the K–W–L sheet (Ogle, 1986). This popular three-columned worksheet helps students prepare for learning by having them (1) list their prior knowledge into a "K" column (what they already Know about the topic), (2) generate a set of questions to search out answers in the "W" column (what I Want to learn about the selected topic), and finally (3) record newly learned information into the "L" column (what new information was Learned about the topic). Even though

Figure 6.1.

Student graphic organizer: Day of the Dead.

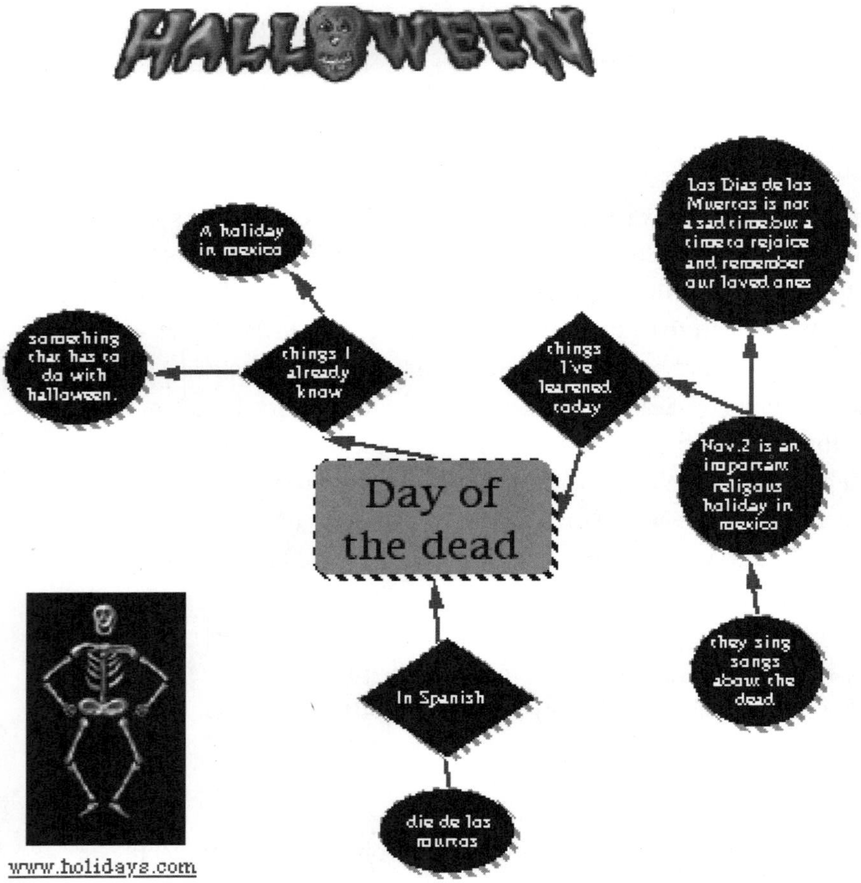

HALLOWEEN

A holiday in mexico

something that has to do with halloween.

things I already know

Las Dias de los Muertos is not a sad time but a time to rejoice and remember our loved ones

things I've learened today

Day of the dead

Nov.2 is an important religous holiday in mexico

In Spanish

they sing songs about the dead

die de los muertos

www.holidays.com

Figure 6.2.

Student graphic organizer: U.S. law.

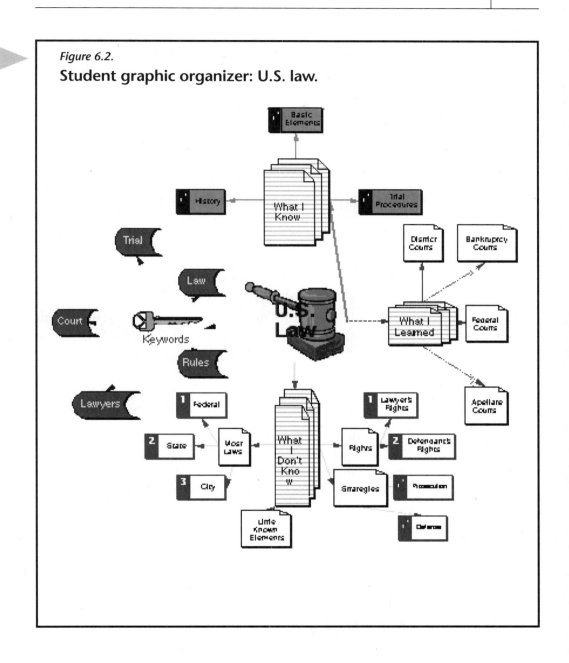

we have the Internet to employ as a teaching and learning tool, there's no reason to give up on older, more traditional tools like the outstanding, pencil-and-paper K–W–L sheet, which provides a simple organizational structure that students can follow when they go to their computers.

Index Cards

Another low-tech activity to prepare students for going out on the Internet on their own is to distribute index cards to the class. Why index cards? Because students love them. Remember being in school and having your teacher give you a bunch of index cards? That magic still works today. When students receive index cards, they know that this activity must be important. Go all out and distribute the pastel-colored cards to really peak their interest.

What do the students do with the index cards? Anything you tell them to, like generating a set of guided focus questions to search for, or recording areas of prior knowledge, or predicting what new information they will find on the Net (see the "folder file folder," Lewin & Shoemaker [1998]).

Using Search Tools Independently

Once they have prepared for their activity using any of the methods just described (or other ones that you have suggested to them), students are ready to go out and do the Free Search. Of course, they need searching skills—how to locate and how to use a search engine or a search directory—that they must already have demonstrated before being given the Free Search assignment. Preliminary Internet skills are those they honed during the Pre- and We Search levels.

Directing Students to Approved Sites

In the last chapter, you read about a variety of search tools that can control student searches by limiting the results. Just as with the We Search, teachers can require students to use search directories such as Yahooligans, KidsClick!, Ask Jeeves for Kids, and Searchopolis, so that the chance of happening upon offensive or inappropriate Web sites is eliminated. Give students the URLs for these relatively safe search tools, and they can begin their Free Search within these approved areas.

Another way to route your Free Searching students to solid search tools is to hyperlink them from a class Web site, a school Web site, or the district's Web site. For example, through links provided at John Mielke's classroom site (http://www.zeeland.k12.mi.us/jmielke/Index.htm) at Zeeland (Michigan) High School, his Free Searching students could choose from seven selected search tools: Yahoo, Google, Intelliseek, NBC, Lycos, and AltaVista. But notice that this teacher menu of search tools includes engines—Go, Google, Intelliseek, Lycos, and AltaVista—that are all excellent searchers; but as they are software-powered (as opposed to human-powered directories), the chances of "false hits," inappropriate hits, and no hits increase. I believe it is worth the chance, though, because students need practice and experience with search engines.

Encourage Variety

As mentioned throughout this book, no single search tool provides complete results all the time. The Web is simply too vast for any one search engine to cover all the sites. Also, Web searchers often grow comfortable (and thus complacent) with the results retrieved from a particular search tool. Strongly suggest to students that they should be proficient in using a number of different search tools, because they will perform better research when they tap into multiple resources. Just as good traditional library research looks at any topic from a variety of points of view, teach your students that Web search tools in themselves represent "points of view," the view of the programmer who has written the software code that tells the search engines how to do their job. Similarly, a search directory represents the view of the people who are creating it—not that that's a bad thing. But points of view can emerge in a variety of fashions, even in electronic media, and students must keep this fact in mind.

HELP!

Remind the students, too, that they can increase their expertise—and make their searching time more worthwhile—when they click on the "Help" button for a quick tutorial on how to operate whatever search tool they are using. Although many of the search tools use basically the same instructions for how to conduct a search, your students will come across research tools that conduct their business differently. Students (and you) should also keep an eye on your favorite search sites for any time they change how the tools provided there are used.

Wasting Time on Typos

The best independent searches and searchers can be brought to a screeching halt if the spelling and typing are not precise. A student researching Vietnam on the Web complained at the end of a class period that, "There is nothing there; I've searched three engines, and none of them had anything on Vietnam." The doubtful teacher asked the student to try again while the teacher watched. Going dutifully to Lycos, the frustrated student typed in the search topic: "Veitnam." An entire class period wasted due to a typo. Many search engines are trying to alleviate this problem by directing searchers to the correct spelling of an incorrectly entered prompt. This sign of progress on the part of the search engines combines elements of good marketing and creative programming.

Suggesting Hits

Another Free Search tip you can offer your students is to help them decide which "hits," or search results, to pursue. Often the number of hits can be quite large, even with a carefully constructed and narrowed search query. How should a student decide which one(s) to check out and which ones to ignore? Picking hits is not an exact science, but here are a few pointers.

First, always read the short blurb that accompanies a hit. For example, when I heard about a cute Web site, created by a witty college student, glorifying orange traffic cones, I was curious to check it out, but I didn't know the site's URL. I did, however, recall the name: Conetastic. So I went to AltaVista's Raging.com engine (http://www.raging.com) and conducted a search. Raging, like Google, loads faster because it isn't a busy portal site with lots of links and information. Raging is just a search engine with a plain, fast-loading look. The first three hits out of 17 that came up searching Raging for Conetastic appear in Figure 6.3.

Hit #1 is the really amusing site I was looking for (http://animation. filmtv.ucla.edu/students/awinfrey/cone.htm), as is obvious from reading the 25-word blurb. (Also, the Web site's name is a match.) The second site's blurb reveals a far different topic, and the third hit provides so little information as to be unintelligible. You should know (and tell your

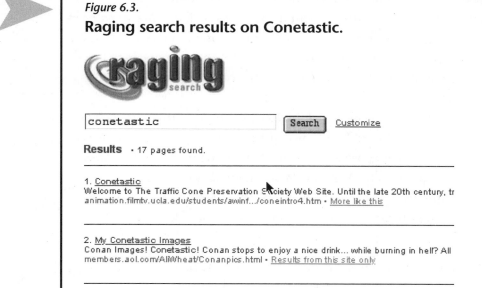

Figure 6.3.

Raging search results on Conetastic.

conetastic   [Search] Customize

Results · 17 pages found.

1. Conetastic
Welcome to The Traffic Cone Preservation Society Web Site. Until the late 20th century, tr
animation.filmtv.ucla.edu/students/awinf.../coneintro4.htm · More like this

2. My Conetastic Images
Conan Images! Conetastic! Conan stops to enjoy a nice drink... while burning in hell? All
members.aol.com/AlWheat/Conanpics.html · Results from this site only

3. Hereeeee's Main
As seen in Yahoo! Internet Life, Digital Diner, TV Guide, Internet Underground, Total TV,
idt.net/~damone/cmain.html · More like this · Results from this site only

Reprinted with permission from AltaVista.

students) that these blurbs are not written by AltaVista's on-call reference librarian (there is no such person), but rather they're simply the first 25 words from the Web site's text. Smart webmasters, then, lead off their sites with accurate—and even catchy—introductions to the information contained on their site. (I use the Conemaster Web site for a fun online training activity. Go to http://trackstar.hprtec.org:80/main/display. php3?option=frames&track_id=13296 to see a place where students can practice their Internet skills. If you'd prefer a shortcut, go to http:// trackstar.hprtec.org and search by author for "Lewin.")

As you learned earlier in the book, search engines prioritize their hits. The software spiders and robots that scour the Web have coded directions for listing the hits in some order, such as the total number of times the key word(s) are at the site, or how many visitors have been to that site, or how many other Web site creators like the searched-for site enough to hyperlink to it. Some search engines will post a percentage next to the hit to inform you, like Northern Light did for my search on "hot water heaters" (see Figure 6.4), what amount of information on the Web site is considered relevant to the search. How it arrives at the percentages is a function of the searcher software robot; the company keeps detailed information private.

A third way to decide which hits to investigate further is to look at the Web sites' domains. In Internet parlance, "domain" refers to the pre-designed code that appears in the URL identifying the type of organization that maintains the Web site. While many new domain names are coming into use (.arts, .inc, .web, .shop, .tv, and so on), the domains most commonly used in Web site addresses are the "old" three-letter codes:

.com   commercial organization (hence the name "dot-coms")
.edu   educational organization
.net   network
.org   nonprofit organization
.gov   government organization

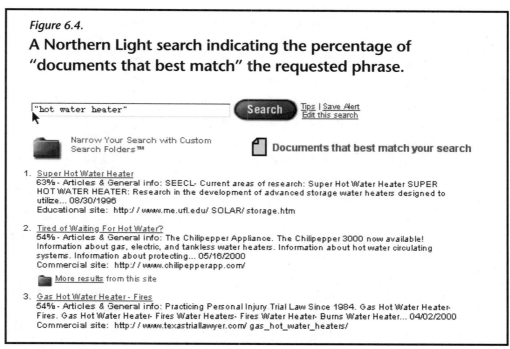

Figure 6.4.

A Northern Light search indicating the percentage of "documents that best match" the requested phrase.

Reprinted with permission of Northern Light, Inc.

Perhaps a site with the ".edu" domain should be checked before a ".com" site. Why? The ".edu" domain indicates that the Web site comes from an educational source, like a public or private school, a college, or a university. These sources can have a better degree of credibility than a ".com" (commercial) site. Notice I wrote "can have" more credibility, not "always have." Many commercial sites, though in the business of making a profit, offer excellent and accurate information. And, conversely, some educational sites, though from a company or organization in the business of increasing knowledge, offer inaccurate or erroneous information. Why would they do this? It's not an intentional act of the part of the educational institution, but it's possible that a professor, graduate student, or undergraduate student posts work on the school's Web site without outside review. Inaccuracies, biases, and even wildly weird stuff can result.

Likewise, an elementary school teacher could post her third graders' research reports on "African mammals" without carefully checking for facts. The result is inaccurate information on the Web waiting for someone else to come along and use it. The ".edu" often means quality control, but not always. The issue of Web site content credibility and the need for students to evaluate that content is addressed in the next section of this chapter.

(A side note on domains. Instruct your students to be very careful about typing the correct domain name, as some unscrupulous webmasters try to take advantage of URL or domain confusion and mistypings. For one of the more notorious examples [and you need not tell your students about this, but perhaps block the site from school access], compare whitehouse.com with whitehouse.gov. A student innocently seeking information about the executive branch of the U.S. federal government who mistakenly goes to whitehouse.com would receive quite a different education indeed!)

The fourth tip for deciding hits to investigate in detail is to go to a few of the most promising sites and preview them. Because the student is hyperlinking to the sites and must wait for them to load into the browser, this previewing can be time-consuming. But once at the actual site, a student can glance over them for a sense of whether something useful may appear. This preview of coming attractions is made easier with a nice feature of the Netscape and Explorer Web browsers: the "Find" command, which allows a student to electronically scan the text of a site looking for a specific word or phrase. Figure 6.5 shows where this "Find" feature resides in Netscape for Mac 4.7 (it's the same for Windows). Internet Explorer calls it "Find on this page" and locates this feature under the [Edit] menu at the top.

Evaluating Web Site Content

Students are thrilled when they locate Web sites that deal with their chosen topics, but they forget that all sites are not created equally. Some sites

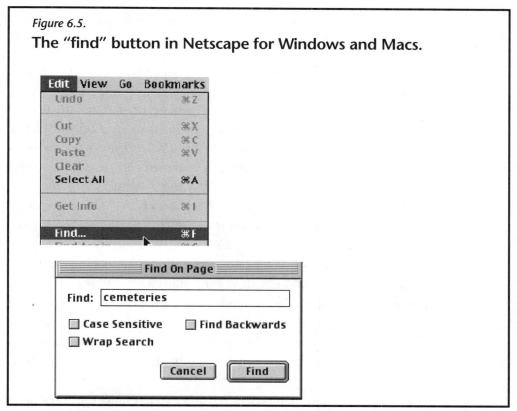

Figure 6.5.
The "find" button in Netscape for Windows and Macs.

Netscape Communicator browser window © 1999 Netscape Communications Corporation. Used with permission. Netscape Communications has not authorized, sponsored, endorsed, or approved this publication and is not responsible for its content.

are excellent resources with accurate information written by credible people, some sites are decent resources, and some sites are the products of dangerously unstable minds.

Internet expert Jamie McKenzie warns students about the dangers of assuming that all information on the Web is accurate, reliable, and useful. It's not. He has written extensively on this subject in his online magazine *From Now On* (http://www.fno.org).

We want our students to be able to tell the difference between reliable and unreliable Web sites. So how do we train our students to be critical consumers of information instead of passive recipients? Try these approaches:

➤ Generate with your students a list of Web site features that instill confidence, such as author's name and e-mail address, bibliographical information on what sources the author used, date of last update of the site's information, a domain address of .edu (educational site), etc. Maybe go to a fun practice site to examine whether it meets the class's criteria for reliability. Try the Mad Science Professor Beakman's 50 Terrific Questions with elementary or middle schoolers (http://www.bonus.com/bonus/list/beakman.right.html). Click on the "Beakman & Jax" link, then on the "50 Questions" link. Be sure to preview them yourself, as some of the questions are quite biologically explicit.

➤ Send high school students to a presearched site that intentionally includes bogus information, such as Ken Umbach's "California's Velcro Crop under Challenge" (http://members.unlimited.net/~kumbach/velcro.html). Also for high school students, consider Vincent Ruggiano's "Feline Reactions to Bearded Men" (http://www.lclark.edu/~ruggiano/netc/Advocacy/bogus/cat.html). Ask the students to evaluate the content reliability.

➤ Send students to Kathy Schrock's "Web Site Evaluation Tools" at her outstanding Web site (http://school.discovery.com/schrockguide/eval.htm). Kathy, a media specialist in Massachusetts, has created surveys for students to fill out while using a site; she presents elementary, middle, and high school versions.

➤ Karen McLachlan, media specialist at East Knox (Ohio) High School has created a scoring rubric with a five-point scale for assessing the content of a Web site (http://cyberbee.com/guide1.html).

➤ Use Internet teacher-trainer Phil Reinhardt's excellent Six Questions method for evaluating the quality of information (http://www.technology4u.com):

1. **What?** What does the article or information say? Does it answer any question (or part of a question) you started with?

2. **Where?** Where is the source of this information? Does it have a person's name, organization name, phone number, e-mail address, site address?

3. **Who?** Who is the author? Can you get in touch?

4. **Why?** Why did the author write this information? What is the purpose? Is there a clear point of view? any bias? any important omissions (missing information)?

5. **When?** When was this information written? Is it current?

6. **Really?** Is there any way to check the accuracy of the information using other sources?

Recording Newly Learned Information During a Free Search

Another required skill for a successful Free Search is that students pay attention while visiting Web sites that offer information on their self-selected topics. What worse scenario for a teacher than being informed at the end of the period that your students "didn't find anything useful"? Imagine them appearing to be busy, productive, and on task at the computers, only to discover that they have little to nothing to show for the time invested. Let's preempt this possibility by requiring that they record notes as they browse the Web. Here are some suggestions for how your students can record the information they find in their Free Search:

➤ Open up an electronic graphic organizer program and multitask by reading information from the Web and paraphrasing it into the graphic organizer.

➤ Open up a word processing program and bring in notes from the Web site, in the same manner as is done with the graphic organizer.

➤ Go low-tech and have students write notes on index cards, yellow sticky notes, or even notebook paper.

Any way that you or the students can devise to help them stay focused and to keep them from forgetting what they learned from Web sites is beneficial.

Of course, note taking opens up another problem: plagiarism. Do your students know the difference between plagiarism and paraphrasing—that is, copying vs. note taking? In these days when moving large sections of text from one site to another is so easily done, digital plagiarism is an obvious and dangerous temptation.

Plagiarism

Imagine that one of your students excitedly finds useful information at a Web site during a Free Search and then merely copies chunks of text and pastes it into a word processing document. The physical act of copying is so easily accomplished these days that it makes old-fashioned word-for-word copying from an encyclopedia seem like a ridiculously cumbersome, antiquated burden. Teachers need to keep a particularly sharp eye out for instances of potential plagiarism because of how easily it can occur. Here are some helpful tips:

➤ If a student's work suddenly seems much improved, be alert. If the writing is far better than you've seen a particular student submit thus far in your class, or if the level of ideas is oddly heightened, ask the student to explain the cause of improvement to you. If necessary, review for all students the difference between paraphrasing/synthesizing and plagiarizing/copying. You might also, for older students, review the concept of "fair use."

➤ When looking at a student's word-processed notes taken from Web resources—and you believe that the notes were merely copied and pasted rather than read and paraphrased—require the student to read the notes aloud to you. Take the mouse and highlight some of the text. If the student has a hard time reading you the notes, then the material was likely copied rather than paraphrased. (One immediate penalty for plagiarized notes is deleting them.) If the student can confidently read the notes aloud to you (some students are particularly good sight readers), you can always have the student "translate" some notes into his or her own words for you. If the student cannot explain or paraphrase the meaning of the notes in her own words, then the comprehension of the notes is insufficient. Again, deletion can be the penalty. Although deletion may seem harsh, the word will get out that you are intolerant of any hint of plagiarism. (You can also explain to your students that as they grow older, the penalties for plagiarism become much more intense: College students can be expelled, and adults writing for publication can be sued.) Of course, you cannot possibly check every student at every computer on every assignment. But you can prioritize certain students for the occasional check. Which students should you be especially interested in monitoring? As an involved teacher, you know who needs it the most.

➤ Visit Rhode Island College's Web site "Plagiarism and Academic Honesty in the Age of Technology" (http://www.ric.edu/library/finding/plagiarism.html). Locate the section on "Web sites that combat plagiarism," and check out some possible help sites.

➤ Consider subscribing to Plagiarism.org (http://www.plagiarism.org). Created by professors at the University of California, plagiarism.org offer a plagiarism checking service. For a fee, you electronically submit suspected student work, and they will run their iAuthenicate® software program to seek exact word matches on other Web sites.

➤ Consider providing an antiplagiarism contract, like the one shown in Figure 6.6 (p. 123).

➤ Require students to properly cite all Web sources. A universally accepted citation form has not yet been determined, but the American Psychological Association (APA) and Modern Language Association (MLA) styles are established. Visit them online: (http://www.apa.org/apa-style/ and http://www.mla.org/www_mla_org/style/style_index.asp?mode=section). Check out Lesley University's (MA) library site for APA style guidance (http://www.lesley.edu/library/guides/citation/apa.html). Debbie Abilock at the Nueva School Library in Hillsborough, California, has a great site with a link to a nifty MLA citation style for students to fill in to cite a Web site (http://www.nueva.pvt.k12.ca.us/ ~debbie/library/research/cit/mla/citwww1.html). Click on "New" NoodleBib, which links to www.noodletools.com.

➤ Require students to attach a printed copy of any Web site they have used in their Free Search. Teacher Jason Shea at Vedder Middle School in Chilliwack, British Columbia, takes no chances. His 8th grade humanities students staple the printed site behind the research report, so if any copying and pasting has occurred, the student has just provided the teacher with the evidence.

When pondering the plagiarism question relative to your own classroom experience, consider the type of assignment you are giving your students: Is it a simple recall type of report, or is it a more involved type of assignment that requires deeper thinking and processing of information? Rudy Avizius, tech administrator for the Maple Shade School District (New Jersey) raised an important point during a presentation I was making. Rudy reminded me that the typical kind of assignment we give students can encourage plagiarism; i.e., "write a report" often means to kids to copy and paste. So he suggests discouraging plagiarism by asking students not merely to regurgitate information, but to process it. This question is also aptly raised by Shari Barnhard at the "Apple Learning Interchange" (ALI) Web site (http://www.ali.apple.com). Click on "K12 Education," then "Forum," and then "Language Arts Round Table." ALI will ask you to register with a sign-in name and password. Then click on "Avoiding Plagiarism." Shari believes the question of digital plagiarism is best addressed up front by asking the right questions for the assignment: Ask students to answer challenging, upper-level-thinking questions. If students are asked to synthesize information and relate it to other lessons, rather than just repeat found information, the chances of plagiarism drop sharply.

Solving Two Final Problems with Free Searches

As students become accustomed to Free Searches, they will learn that not all time spent looking at the Internet is necessarily constructive. Two problems that all Internet users encounter—inside and outside the classroom—are wandering and insufficiency of resources.

Figure 6.6.

Anti-Plagiarism Contract

Name: _____ Date: _____

Anti-Plagiarism Contract
Assignment #1
1B English

Define plagiarism:

_____
_____
_____
_____

Source for this definition:

_____
_____
_____
_____

I, _____ , understand the meaning of
Plagiarism. With this understanding, I am also **completely conscious of the consequences**
that an act of plagiarism will have on my academic standing. Therefore, I agree to refrain
from plagiarizing the work that I submit in this course.

_____

Student signature and date

_____

Parent/Guardian signature and date

_____

Teacher signature and date

Created by Angela Andréa Hernandez Sepulveda and Camila Krug, Edmonton, Alberta, Canada (while
teaching at Instituto Tecnologico y de Studios Superiores de Monterey, Mexico).

Wandering

With freedom to use the Web, some students will intentionally (or by chance) wander from useful, appropriate sites into areas that are either off their topic or inappropriate. Just as with the We Search, some solutions can help stop wandering from occurring during a Free Search.

➤ Make all students sign an Acceptable Use Policy (AUP) that clearly specifies the expectations for proper Internet behavior and the consequences for misuse.

➤ Use your Web browser's tracking devices. Netscape has a [Go] command that reveals a list of recently visited sites and a [History] command; Explorer has a [Go] command and a [History] beneath it. Students who know you are likely to check the history of their usage probably will not risk discovery by going to prohibited sites.

➤ Teach students how to "bookmark" selected Web sites. Netscape will automatically save a site's URL when you select the menu button [Bookmark] and click on [Add a Bookmark]. Explorer calls them "favorites" and uses the same procedure. The network gurus at some schools, however, don't like having hundreds or thousands of bookmarks stored in the school's computers. So you can send students to a Web site that will store them free of charge. One such site is "My Bookmarks" (http://www.mybookmarks.com); another is "Murl" (http://www.murl.com/splash/). Besides freeing hard drive space on the school's computers, this approach adds flexibility; students can access their bookmarks or favorites from any computer with a Web connection—from home or from a different computer in the lab, if anyone needs to be moved.

➤ Install network software that allows the teacher to monitor student Internet use.

Insufficient Sources

Students are thrilled to find a great Web site with information on their chosen topic. But they sometimes forget that information from only a single source (whether an "old media" source, like an encyclopedia or magazine, or a high-tech source, like a Web site) does not suffice for a quality research project. To keep students focused on finding enough information to support (or verify) their research, consider the following solutions:

➤ Require students to conduct Web searches with more than one search tool. If, for example, a student has asked Excite's search engine for sites on "capital punishment," and the student found only one useful site on the topic, then the student should try another search tool: HotBot, InfoSeek, or AltaVista, or a specialized site, perhaps one from the legal profession or a law library. Students need to understand that each search engine has its own database, so the results of even simple searches will vary from searcher to searcher.

➤ Consider having students use a meta-search tool like Dogpile (http://www.dogpile.com), MetaCrawler (http://www.metacrawler.com), Search.com (http://www.search.com) (formerly Savvy Search), or Intelliseek (http://www.profusion.com). These meta-search sites simultaneously consult multiple engines for your topic. The positive side to a meta-search is how many suggested sites you receive on your topic. The downside is the reverse of the same coin: So many hits can overwhelm students.

Conclusion

The focus of this book has been on the practical: how to take this vast resource, the Internet and its World Wide Web, and make it a practical instructional ally. With so much information (and misinformation) available to schools with a mere mouse click, you need to learn how to narrow the horde of possibilities down into something useful to your teaching and to your students' learning.

This book has also been about structure: how to structure student experience on the Web to keep it educationally sound. As opposed to the "turn 'em loose" approach to Web use, I have presented a structured three-level approach—Pre-Search, We Search, and Free Search—to allow us, the teachers, to control the flow in order to ensure educational success.

Please keep in touch. Send me your thoughts, lessons, student samples, and your favorite Web sites. The Internet is here to stay, and teachers need each other to help make it work for the students and the parents who entrust to us their children's education.

References

Lewin, L., & Shoemaker, B. J. (1998). *Great performances: Creating classroom-based assessment tasks*. Alexandria, VA: Association for Supervision and Curriculum Development.

Ogle, D. (1986). K–W–L: A Teaching Model That Develops Active Reading of Expository Text. *The Reading Teacher, 39*, 564.

Glossary

Archie is an older means of finding files for downloading via FTP. Many files can now be found through search engines on the Web.

Browser is a program used to find specific sites on the Internet, usually on the Web. Netscape and Microsoft Internet Explorer are examples of browsers.

Cyberspace is the virtual reality where e-mail is exchanged, Web pages distributed, and packets lost. Also, the placeholder of culture on the Internet.

Ethernet is one method of connecting computers into a network. Ethernet comes in two types: 10Base-T and ThinNet. ThinNet is a coaxial version that is commonly employed as a backbone network. 10Base-T is used in a star configuration connected to hubs; it is often used in computer labs.

FAQ stands for frequently asked questions. Most topics about the Internet have been summarized in FAQ. These are helpful guides for using the tools and services available on the Internet.

Flame is the term for sending angry or nasty messages over the Internet.

FTP stands for File Transfer Protocol. It lets users share files over the Internet. Most FTP servers allow anonymous login; that is, they permit any user to log in to access files, such as system updates and shareware.

Gopher is a text-based, hierarchical menu system for navigating through text files on the Internet. It was ideal in 1992, but is now obsolete.

HTML stands for Hypertext Markup Language; it is the language of the World Wide Web. All Web pages are composed in HTML, which is what the browser reads as it downloads a page to be assembled into pictures, texts, and links.

HTTP stands for Hypertext Transfer Protocol. It is the protocol, or language, that Web servers and Web browsers speak.

Init String is the set of characters that configures or initializes a modem in preparation for making a connection. Most modems come with their own unique Init String.

Internet is a collection of networks. Each local area network is connected to a wide area network, which is then connected to a regional network. The Internet is a network of all these networks.

IRC stands for Internet Relay Chat. It is the common meeting place for chatting on the Internet. In IRC, users establish channels where others join in for live conversation.

ISP stands for Internet Service Provider. ISPs provide users connections to the Internet via dial-up modems. AOL, for example, is an ISP.

kbps stands for kilobytes per second. It denominates the speed of a modem; e.g., 28 kbps. The higher the number, the faster the modem and, therefore, the faster the Internet connection.

LAN stands for Local Area Network, usually a connection among computers in a single office or a single building.

Listserv is a computer that manages an e-mail mailing list. When someone posts a message to a listserv, or mailing list, this computer makes sure everyone on the list gets a copy.

Modem stands for modulator/demodulator. It is a device that allows your computer to communicate with another computer over a telephone line. The modem translates the signal from digital to analog for transmission, and from analog to digital for reception.

Netiquette is Internet etiquette. These are the rules of courtesy that all users should follow. For example, do not send e-mail typed in all capitals because it seems like shouting.

Netscape is a specific Web browser; another is Microsoft Explorer.

POP/SMTP are protocols for sending e-mail. POP stands for Post Office Protocol, and SMTP stands for Simple Mail Transfer Protocol.

PPP/SLIP are two types of protocol for connecting to an Internet provider. PPP stands for Point-to-Point Protocol, and SLIP stands for Serial Line Internet Protocol.

Protocol is a standardized system, or code, for transmitting digital messages or data. A number of protocols are used for different purposes.

Search engine is a program that scans the contents of a great many Web sites to find information requested by the user. Google, Lycos, and HotBot are examples of search engines.

Server is a central computer that provides service to a network, such as receiving and distributing files, and storing programs and data. The server is controlled by the other computers on the network.

Spam is a derogatory term for unwanted messages, usually advertisements, distributed indiscriminately to a large number of addresses.

TCP/IP stands for Transmission Control Protocol/Internet Protocol. These are the standard Ethernet protocols for Internet communications.

Telnet is a method of remotely connecting a user to a computer from another site. It permits sharing of expensive computer resources over long distances via the Internet.

URL stands for Uniform Resource Locator. It is the string of characters, or "address," that references a specific Web site or other Internet resource.

Usenet newsgroup is a collection of messages from all over the Internet relating to a single topic. These newsgroups allow users to get information on a specific topic from other users with the same interest.

WAN stands for Wide Area Network, usually a connection among local area networks or among separate locations.

WWW stands for the World Wide Web. A URL that includes the characters WWW is the address of a site on the Web.

Source: Adapted from *The Networked Educator,* http://www.teleport.com. Used with permission.

INDEX

Page references followed by *f* refer to
figures.

About the Author

Larry Lewin has been a classroom teacher for 24 years at the elementary, middle, and high school levels. On leave from his Eugene, Oregon, School District, he consults nationally on educational topics of interest, including Classroom-Based Performance Assessment, Integrating the Internet into Instruction, and Reading Across the Curriculum with Comprehension Attack Strategies.

First interested in the potentials of the Internet in the mid-1990s, he has spent six years working it into his instructional repertoire. Many of the examples, ideas, and techniques found in this book come from his experimentation; other ideas he has gratefully acquired from other teachers in the U.S. and Canada.

The "name of the game" for Larry is, and has always been, how to deputize this vast resource into an instructional assistant. As great as the Internet is, it is not smart enough to teach our students. But Larry shows us how we can confidently use it to support our teaching.

Larry is the coauthor, with Betty Jean Shoemaker, of ASCD's book *Great performances: Creating classroom-based assessment tasks*, published in 1999. He also authored writing process textbooks for the Stack the Deck Writing Program, and he has published articles in *Educational Leadership, The Reading Teacher, Language Arts, Middle Ground,* and *Multimedia Schools.*

He lives in Eugene, Oregon, with his wife Linda and their dog Rudy.

He is willing to leave them periodically to provide workshop presentations for school districts. He can be reached at

Larry Lewin   Phone: 541-343-1577
2145 Lincoln St.   E-mail: llewin@teleport.com and
                                 larry@larrylewin.com
Eugene, OR 97405   Web sites: http://www.teleport.com/~llewin and
                                 http://www.larrylewin.com

Related ASCD Resources: Technology and the Internet

Audiotapes

Differentiation for the 21st Century: Technology as a Teaching Tool, by Linda Brandon and Sally Simon (#201206)

Integrating Technology Into Schools: Developing a Technology Plan That Works, by Rick Harrell (#298085)

The Internet and Brain-Based Learning: A Powerful Team, by Kim Lindey and Kristen Nelson (#201128)

Technology Grant Writing Toolbox, by Mary Francis Zilonis (#200194)

Using Technology Raises Student Test Scores, by Susan Giancola (#201122)

CD-ROM and Multimedia

Educational Leadership on CD-ROM, 1992–98 (1 hybrid CD-ROM) (#598223)

Make It Happen: Inquiry and Technology in the Middle School Curriculum Program, by Judith Zorfass (#097161)

Online Resources

Visit ASCD's Web site (www.ascd.org) for the following professional development opportunities:

Online Tutorials (http://www.ascd.org/frametutorials.html)

Professional Development Online: *Planning for Technology,* by Vicki Hancock (http://www.ascd.org/framepdonline.html) (for a small fee; password protected)

Print Products

Curriculum/Technology Quarterly (Spring 2001): Technology for the Visual and Performing Arts (#101054)

Curriculum/Technology Quarterly (Winter 2000): Technology for Foreign Language Study (#101053)

Educational Leadership: Teaching the Information Generation (Vol. 58, No. 2, October 2000) (#100284)

Design Tools for the Internet-Supported Classroom, by Judi Harris (#198009)

Learning with Technology: 1998 ASCD Yearbook, edited by Chris Dede (#198000)

Visual Tools for Constructing Knowledge (#196072) by David Hyerle.

Videotapes

The Lesson Collection: Tape 14: Environmental Project—Internet (Middle School) (#400066)

Teaching and Learning with New Technologies: Teaching and Learning with the Internet: 2 Videos (#496047)

For additional information, visit us on the World Wide Web (http://www.ascd.org), send an e-mail message to member@ascd.org, call the ASCD Service Center (1-800-933-ASCD or 703-578-9600, then press 2), send a fax to 703-575-5400, or write to Information Services, ASCD, 1703 N. Beauregard St., Alexandria, VA 22311-1714 USA.